POWERFUL
PEOPLE SKILLS

HOW TO FORM, BUILD AND MAINTAIN STRONGER,
LONG-LASTING RELATIONSHIPS

ST Training Solutions
Success Skills Series

HEATHER HANSEN

POWERFUL
PEOPLE SKILLS

HOW TO FORM, BUILD AND MAINTAIN STRONGER, LONG-LASTING RELATIONSHIPS

Marshall Cavendish
Business

Published by Marshall Cavendish Business
An imprint of Marshall Cavendish International
1 New Industrial Road, Singapore 536196

Other Marshall Cavendish Offices
Marshall Cavendish Ltd. 5th Floor 32–38 Saffron Hill, London EC1N 8FH · Marshall Cavendish Corporation. 99 White Plains Road, Tarrytown NY 10591-9001, USA · Marshall Cavendish International (Thailand) Co Ltd. 253 Asoke, 12th Flr, Sukhumvit 21 Road, Klongtoey Nua, Wattana, Bangkok 10110, Thailand · Marshall Cavendish (Malaysia) Sdn Bhd, Times Subang, Lot 46, Subang Hi-Tech Industrial Park, Batu Tiga, 40000 Shah Alam, Selangor Darul Ehsan, Malaysia

Marshall Cavendish is a trademark of Times Publishing Limited

National Library Board Singapore Cataloguing in Publication Data
Hansen, Heather.
   Powerful people skills / Heather Hansen. – Singapore : Marshall Cavendish Business,
     c2009.
   p. cm. – (Success skills series)
   Includes index.
   ISBN-13 : 978-981-261-854-2

   1. Interpersonal relations. 2. Communication in organizations.
   3. Interpersonal communication. I. Title. II. Series: Success skills series (ST Training
   Solutions)

HF5386
650.13 — dc22   OCN386813122

Printed in Singapore by Times Printers Pte Ltd

ACKNOWLEDGEMENTS

When writing a book on relationships, it's close to impossible to mention all the people who have influenced, inspired and supported me in so many ways. Lessons learnt from everyone I've met appear throughout these pages, and those who know me well will recognise familiar stories.

I would like to extend my sincere gratitude to my many friends, colleagues and clients, in Singapore and abroad, who have supported both me and my business, and from whom I've learnt at least as much as I've taught, and in many cases much more.

Special thanks to my mom, Patsy Torvend, for instilling in me a love of learning from a very early age, and for her support, input and especially patience as I worked on final revisions during almost her entire visit to Singapore. Thank you to my dad, Thom Torvend, and his wife Robyn, for their interest and excitement about the book from start to finish.

I'd like to thank my good friends and family: Tony Maxwell for his help in brainstorming titles and working on my author bio; Alison Lester for keeping me sane; Sam Jarman for his continued interest in my many endeavours; and Palle and Birthe Hansen for their pride in all I do.

A very special thank you goes to Shirley Taylor for giving me the opportunity to be part of such a fantastic series. As Series Editor, her attention to detail has improved this book tenfold. Thank you for your commitment, encouragement and most importantly, your friendship.

I'd also like to extend my thanks to the entire team at Marshall Cavendish, especially my editor, Mindy Pang, for her tireless work on this text. A huge thank you to Edwin Ng as well, for reading my mind and bringing this book to life with his fantastic illustrations.

And finally, thank you to my wonderful husband, Peter, for his unending support, encouragement, patience and love, and to my darling daughter, Victoria, for brightening my life and always making me smile.

DEDICATION

To my daughter, Victoria, with love.
May all your relationships be powerful.

PREFACE

Congratulations on picking up this copy of *Powerful People Skills*. I'm very proud that this is one of the first books in the ST Training Solutions Success Skills series. This series includes several short, practical books on a range of topics that will help you develop your skills and enhance your success at work and in your personal life too.

The Success Skills series was originally created to meet the needs of participants of ST Training Solutions public workshops. After attending our workshops, many participants expressed a real desire to continue learning, to find out more about the topic, to take it to another level. They were hungry for knowledge. Just the effect I hoped for when I set up ST Training Solutions in 2007. With the Success Skills series of books, the experience and expertise of our trainers can be enjoyed by many more people.

As Series Editor, I've enjoyed working with the authors to make sure the books are easy-to-read, highly practical, and written in straightforward, simple language. Every book is packed with essential tools and strategies that will make you more effective and successful. We've included illustrations throughout that reinforce some key points, because I believe we learn more if we add some fun and humour. You'll also notice some key features that highlight important learning points:

Myth Buster Here you will find a statement that is not true, with notes on the true facts of the matter.

Fast Fact Useful snippets of information or special points to remember.

Aha! Moment

This is a 'light bulb' moment, when we note something you may be able to conclude from a discussion. Don't forget to note your own 'Aha! Moments' perhaps when you receive some extra insight that clarifies an important point.

Try This

Here you'll find a suggestion for how you can put a special point into practice, either at home or at work.

Danger Zone

You'll find some words of warning here, such as things to avoid or precautions to take.

Star Tips

At the end of each chapter you'll find a list of Star Tips — important notes to remind you about the key points.

By picking up this book you have already shown a desire to learn more. The solid advice and practical guidelines provided in this book will show you how you can really go from good to great!

Good luck!

Shirley Taylor

Shirley Taylor
Series Editor
CEO, ST Training Solutions Pte Ltd

ST Training Solutions

www.shirleytaylortraining.com
www.shirleytaylor.com

Shape the Star in You!

Visit www.STSuccessSkills.com now to download your free e-book **'Your 7 Steps to Success'** containing motivating advice from our Success Skills authors. You can also read lots of author articles and order the latest titles in the Success Skills series.

CONTENTS

INTRODUCTION

I'm sure you've met those people who seem to get along well with everyone. They always have something interesting to say. They close the best deals, land the biggest clients and quickly work their way up the professional ladder. Are these people just born natural communicators with magnetic personalities? Do they have something you don't, or know some secret to being popular and successful? Absolutely not. They've simply mastered the process of interacting effectively with others. They know how to click with people from the first time they meet, and understand the importance of maintaining their relationships for the long term.

I've spent my entire adult life travelling internationally, meeting new people, learning new cultures and re-establishing myself in different places. I've worked numerous jobs, established two businesses and even started a family in a foreign land. Many of my friends say they could never imagine living so far away from home, and they wonder how I do it. Of course I miss my friends and family, but there is much truth to the adage, 'Home is where the heart is'.

To feel at home no matter where I am in the world, I've learnt how to make new friends. It's as simple as that. My old friends are always in my heart and I carry them with me wherever I go. Thanks to modern technology, I can maintain strong relationships with them in ways that would not have been possible ten, or even five, years ago. I also understand that my personal happiness (and professional success) is dependent on applying powerful people skills in order to form, build and maintain new and meaningful relationships wherever I may be. Luckily I've found that there are great people everywhere, and it's really just a matter of approaching new relationships with an open mind and heart.

You might not be doing something as drastic as starting a business overseas, but you're still faced with situations regularly where you have to apply some interpersonal intelligence. You need to interact with clients and customers, colleagues and bosses, and family and friends. Depending on the strength of these relationships, you'll either enjoy the interactions or you'll dread them.

Making friends isn't as easy as our kindergarten days when we could go up to someone in the playground and ask, "Will you be my friend?" As adults, we complicate matters with our judgements and expectations of others. Plus, we carry that heavy, debilitating stuff called 'baggage'. We've been hurt by the people who have said (figuratively or literally), "No, actually, I don't want to be your friend." We've embarrassed ourselves by saying or doing foolish things, and we swear we'll never make those mistakes again. We lose confidence and our self-esteem suffers. As a result, we end up holding ourselves back from taking chances to achieve great things and meet caring people who can help us along the way.

That's my motivation for writing this book — to help you overcome any shortcoming you may think you have that is holding you back from forming stronger, long-lasting and powerful relationships personally and professionally. I'll take you step-by-step from preparing for new relationships and building your confidence in meeting new people, to how to click with them from the moment you meet. You'll learn how to apply powerful interpersonal skills such as active listening and great conversational techniques to further enhance your relationships.

And let's not forget the relationships you've already built! I'll show you winning ways to maintain those relationships and keep them strong and enjoyable. We'll also look at how technology is changing the way we interact in our relationships on a global scale. And since our world is getting smaller and smaller, I'll show you how to manage cross-cultural relationships confidently and successfully.

I hope the lessons and techniques you learn in this book will give you greater confidence in your interactions with others and enable you to make the most of all your relationships.

Enjoy your life and the people you share it with!

Heather Hansen
www.HansenSLT.com

ASSESS YOURSELF

How powerful are your people skills?

1.   Which of the following are people skills?

a)   Active listening.

b)   Mirroring and matching body language.

c)   Harmonising my voice and tone with others.

d)   Knowing how to read and empathise with the feelings of others.

e)   All of the above.

2.   How do you prepare for new relationships?

a)   I put on a good attitude and a great smile.

b)   I think about the type of people I want to meet and only focus on them.

c)   I make sure I have a strong relationship with myself.

d)   Uh... Should I be preparing myself for relationships?

e)   a and c.

3.   To build and maintain strong relationships, you must first have:

a)   Trust

b)   Open communication

c)   Respect

d)   All of the above

4. The best way to build rapport when you meet someone is to:

a) Agree with everything they say.

b) Laugh at their jokes so they feel more comfortable.

c) Take a sincere interest in them.

d) Impress them with your large vocabulary.

5. When you forget someone's name:

a) Just pretend you didn't and avoid instances where you might have to use it.

b) Admit it and immediately ask for the name.

c) Keep talking and hope the name comes to you.

d) Avoid the person completely so you don't have to be in an awkward situation.

6. Asking lots of questions is the best way to show someone that you are interested in them and can keep the conversation going.

a) True

b) False

7. Your voice and tone are important in building rapport because:

a) People have expectations as to how you should sound.

b) You need to know how to harmonise with the people you meet.

c) Poor voice control can make you annoying to listen to.

d) All of the above.

8. Online friendships can be enhanced by:

a) Keeping in touch regularly.

b) Being as open and honest as you would be offline.

c) Having a giving attitude and sharing your knowledge.

d) All of the above.

9. Which of the following are ways you can use your body to communicate:

a) Use facial expressions

b) Fidget

c) Change your posture

d) All of the above

e) a and c

10. Successful people were born with powerful people skills.

a) True

b) False

How did you do?

1. If you answered (e), then you are absolutely right. These are just four of the many powerful people skills you'll learn in this book. Active listening techniques will be covered in Chapter 4, body language in Chapter 5, voice and tone in Chapter 6, and empathy in Chapter 3.

2. The correct answer is (e) again. If you didn't think it was necessary to prepare for new relationships, turn to Chapter 2 to learn why this is such an important step.

3. Yet again, your answer should be (e). We'll cover these points and other ways to maintain strong relationships in Chapter 9.

4. Taking an interest in others (answer c) is the best way for you to quickly build rapport. We'll talk about the many ways you can click with people in Chapter 3.

5. The correct way to get out of this awkward situation is (b). Learn how to dodge, or recover from, difficult situations like this in Chapter 8.

6. Many people think the correct answer is (a), but it is actually (b). Turn to Chapters 4 and 7 to learn how to listen actively and carry on great conversations without resorting to interrogation techniques.

7. Your voice is just as important as your appearance, so the correct answer is (d). You'll learn how to use your voice and tone effectively in Chapter 6.

8. The correct answer to this question is also (d). Chapter 10 will give you detailed tips for building and maintaining online relationships.

9. Although fidgeting might be a negative signal to send with your body, it's still a way in which you communicate with visual cues. Therefore the correct answer is (d). You'll learn all about how to read body language and send your own visual messages in Chapter 5.

10. The answer to this statement is definitely (b). In Chapter 1, you will discover how people learn and apply people skills to become more successful both personally and professionally.

PEOPLE SKILLS
IN PERSPECTIVE

"No man is an island,
entire of itself..."

John Donne

What are people skills?

When I ask this question of my workshop participants I always get some variation of the answer: 'communicating and building relationships with others'. It's true that this is what people skills help us to do, but they aren't really the skills themselves.

Let's dig a little deeper. If we want to 'communicate and build relationships with others', what specific skills do we need? This is a more challenging question because many people believe that a person is simply born a good communicator, or naturally likeable or blessed with a great personality. This is not actually the case. Many don't realise there are learnable skills that can help you achieve these things.

When I was young, I used to love stories about children brought up in the wild, such as Tarzan, Mowgli (from Rudyard Kipling's *The Jungle Book*), and Romulus and Remus (the supposed founders of Rome). Legends describe these children as being highly developed and in some ways more advanced than you and me. Not only do they retain their capabilities to integrate successfully into human society, they also possess highly developed animal senses.

In reality, however, the few documented cases (at least those not believed to be hoaxes) show that children who grow up without human contact are actually quite retarded in their emotional and mental development and their ability to interact with other humans. Without the enculturation that occurs in normal human society, these children are not able to develop an understanding of interpersonal relationships. They do not have interpersonal needs because they have adapted to a world without them. Just as we wouldn't know the first thing about surviving among wolves or monkeys, these children have no idea how to interact with people.

 Aha! Moment

I am not born with people skills. I learn them from my parents, teachers and, most importantly, the people I choose to build relationships with.

When faced with the exciting yet challenging situation of meeting new people, there are several skills you will need. First and foremost, you'll need some confidence and a great attitude in order to go up to strangers and introduce yourself. You'll want to present yourself well and send out a professional image. You'll need to know how to read the situation and the other person, and then know what to say and how to say it so that you can 'click' with that person and carry on an interesting conversation. You'll want to be able to listen actively to your new contact and respond appropriately. Then, assuming things go well, you'll need to know how to keep the necessary contact to maintain your new relationship.

These are all people skills, and by studying them you will be able to improve your relationships and achieve greater success in your life. You'll find the techniques to get you there throughout the pages of this book.

Try This

What would your life be like if you could improve your people skills? Take a moment to think about how your life could change if you apply the lessons you learn here. Could you have a better job, more confidence, be more popular or achieve greater success? What goals would you like to achieve?

Lessons from successful people

We all know people who seem to be able to work a room effortlessly. They get along well with everyone and always have something incredibly interesting to say. People are drawn to them and want to help them any way they can. They are usually the most successful people we know. These people have many things in common:

- **They are confident and self-assured.** They are able to enter into healthy relationships because, above all, they have a good relationship with themselves.

- **They know how to make you feel better about yourself.** That's why you like them. By taking a sincere interest in your needs, they make you feel comfortable and cared for.

- **They are authentic.** Because they believe in their own worth and ability to add something to our world, they share themselves openly with others. They have nothing to hide and give freely to those around them.

- **They are respectful.** Even with all the power and success in the world, they value people and have complete respect for humanity.

- **They are honest in their dealings with others.** This helps to build trusting relationships.

- **They are positive.** They attract positive people and opportunities towards them.

- **Their messages are clear on every level.** There is no hidden agenda in their voice, words or body language.

The bottom line is that successful individuals understand the power of people skills and value their relationships with others. They don't have a magic wand or a secret code. They've simply learnt powerful lessons for interpersonal success and have then applied them to their interactions with others.

Many people make the mistake of thinking that successful individuals have accomplished everything on their own. We talk about *self-made men* and *self-made millionaires*, but do you really think men like American property mogul, Donald Trump, or the ruler of the Virgin empire, Richard Branson, achieved their huge successes on their own? Not a chance. They've had the help and support of numerous people along the way, and they've gained that support because they've built strong relationships. They have powerful people skills!

Fast Fact

Richard Branson is dyslexic and actually did rather poorly in school. His strength and popularity lies in how he connects with and motivates people.

Myth Buster

I don't need anyone's help to succeed. I'm better off on my own anyway!

The belief that you can 'go it alone' (or would be better off that way) is misguided and arrogant. Two heads are always better than one. If you pull on the strengths of your relationships and lean on others for support, you lighten your burden and can achieve much more as a result.

The chain of influence

Every individual you meet has some affect on the direction of your life, the choices you make, and ultimately your degree of success. Even unsuccessful relationships have changed who you are and continue to influence how you act and react to different people and situations. People who you wish could have played a larger role in your life have also influenced you through their absence.

Your relationships join together to create what I call a 'chain of influence'. Starting with your parents or caregivers, you have been led and directed to other people and opportunities through each of them. If you removed a link from your chain, your life would probably be very different.

To illustrate this point, let's take a look at the relationships that have led to me writing this book and have greatly influenced its content. Since this is a book on relationships, every relationship I've ever had has made its way into these pages through lessons learnt, but let's just focus on the most important people who have had a hand in making this book a reality.

No matter the experience or accomplishment, my parents were the first and most important influences in my life. Our caregivers play the greatest role in our early lives and development. They choose the schools we go to and where we spend our childhood. They also provide us with our first lessons in interpersonal relationships.

My parents' choice of schooling led me to meet numerous teachers who planted seeds about writing and expressing ideas. My eighth grade English teacher, Mrs. Wilburn, piqued my interest in the importance of English grammar, while my high school speech coach, Ron Underwood, taught me how to organise my thoughts for the greatest impact. I never would have dreamt of writing a book until two of my college professors, Dr. Barb West and Dr. Brian Klunk, mentioned separately that they thought I would do well in academics and research. They could see me spreading knowledge and writing books. I always remembered those comments. Although I didn't choose the academic route, they gave me the confidence to pursue training and writing.

Also during my time at university, my guidance counsellor and German professor, Dr. Mike Sharp, encouraged me to pursue an additional degree in the German language and was instrumental in arranging an internship for me in Switzerland. That happens to be where I met my husband, Peter.

Peter has obviously played an incredible role in this book since our relationship is one of the most important in my life today, if not *the* most important. Additionally, it was Peter's work that brought me to Singapore and put me in the position to meet the people who would have the most immediate impact on this project. About two years ago, I went to a conference here where I met my good friend, Ricky Lien. We had many things in common and immediately clicked. He was one of the first to take me under his wing and show me the ropes here in Singapore. And he was the one who introduced me to his friend and colleague, Shirley Taylor.

The rest is history. Shirley was forming a new training company (ST Training Solutions) just as I was looking for an organiser for my public workshops. She took on my programmes, began organising my seminars and marketing me to her clients. When she was offered the opportunity to be editor for a series of business books, she immediately asked if I'd like to get involved. She introduced me to the publisher and their team of fantastic people behind the scenes that make a project like this possible. Without her, you wouldn't be holding this book in your hands.

What if just one link in this chain had been missing? What if Dr. Sharp hadn't been my guidance counsellor? Would I have ever met my husband? What if I hadn't met Ricky? Would I have met Shirley? It's possible, but it may have been much later and under different circumstances. I never could have guessed that my chain of influence would lead me to this point today.

Aha! Moment

Every relationship in my life is important. Without one of them, I would be a different person, and my life would be on a different course. Equally powerful is the effect I have on others' lives — often without even knowing it.

Try This

Think about a positive experience in your life or one of your greatest achievements. Who are the people that contributed to making that happen? Starting with your parents and the decisions they made for you, and working all the way up to the experience itself, create your own chain of influence.

Relationships and opportunities

In addition to influencing the course of our lives, our friends, family members and colleagues also present us with new opportunities that help us to advance socially and professionally. I don't know about you, but I like doing business with people I like. I could give you several examples of situations where I have paid significantly more for a pretty common service because I had built a relationship and enjoyed working with that particular service provider. What's more, when I'm happy with a service, I talk about it — a lot. I offer these great people additional business through my circle of contacts.

Myth Buster

I don't have time to meet new people and don't need any more friends. I'm happy with who I've got.

This belief holds you back from reaching your potential. You don't have to form deep relationships with everyone you meet. Even when you are happy and comfortable with the friends you have, meeting new people can lead to new opportunities both socially and professionally.

On a personal level, building friendships can open doors to entirely new social circles. Let's say you just met Erika and you both really hit it off. You'll most likely want to invite her to meet your other friends and she will do the same with you. You never know who you might meet. Maybe someone in Erika's circle of friends is looking for a tennis partner just like you are, has children the same ages as yours, or works in the same industry and knows of a job opportunity you might be interested in.

If influence and opportunity aren't reason enough to place more value on your relationships, then consider your own happiness. I love to have meetings with people in the morning because it really gets my day going. I find conversations with colleagues and good friends incredibly stimulating, and I get a boost from all the great ideas we discuss. Due to the time difference between Singapore (where I live) and California (where I'm from), I usually call my good friends and family in the early morning so I can catch them before they sit down for dinner the night before. What a great way to start my day!

Interpersonal needs

Having great conversations with people who are close to you can be such an energising experience because, through this process, you are fulfilling your interpersonal needs. This is one gas tank that you can't fill through self-service. You're going to need the help of your friends to feel full again on an interpersonal level.

Fast Fact

Relationships are based on balancing our own interpersonal needs with another's. Problems arise in our relationships when our expectations aren't met and our interpersonal needs aren't fulfilled.

Even great relationships can be complicated. It doesn't matter how much you *click*, *mesh*, or *gel*, everyone is different and there will always be compromises to be made. Nevertheless, we will still form relationships time and time again in order to fulfil our interpersonal needs.

William Schutz outlined three basic interpersonal needs in a study he conducted in 1958. I feel these are still very relevant today:

Inclusion

Affection

Control

Let's take a closer look at each of these needs.

1. Inclusion

We are all looking for acceptance and inclusion from others. This is not only true on a group scale, such as in your workplace or a trade association, but also in your dealings with specific individuals in your life. We want to feel that our friends and colleagues agree with our decisions, support our actions and accept us as equal, contributing members to the group or relationship.

Relationships can get rocky when you feel your friend or colleague doesn't include you. If your good friend makes an important decision or does something new and exciting without having ever told you about it, you might feel the sudden pang that comes from being left out. The same is true in group situations. There's often an awkward stage when you join a new club and feel like the lonely outsider. In the workplace, these feelings could come out if you aren't included in meetings or if no one asks your opinion on an important issue.

2. Affection

Depending on the individual and the relationship, a person's need for affection and to feel cared for on a personal level will change. Even in professional relationships, you probably want to feel as though people care about you and your welfare. Affection doesn't have to be in a romantic sense. It can also be shown through the support and encouragement you're given on a professional level.

In personal relationships, our need for affection is much stronger. We have the expectation that our friends and family love and support us in everything we do, and despite what we do. Some people may need more support and encouragement than others, and it's important to be sensitive to that. Being able to empathise with others is an essential skill, and we'll look closely at this in Chapter 3.

3. Control

Even though our lives are interdependent and we need each other in order to thrive, it is still important that we feel a degree of autonomy and control over our own lives and circumstances. Some people will need to have a lot of control in their relationships to feel fulfilled. Others are perfectly happy taking a more passive approach and letting other people lead.

In professional settings, where some people are formally granted more control and power than others, these needs hang in a delicate balance. As we'll see in Chapter 9, an abuse of power can quickly ruin relationships. Managers in particular need to be aware of their staff's need for autonomy and the power to make decisions. They need to feel as though they play an active role in the direction of the organisation.

Every individual will be influenced to a greater or lesser degree by each of these needs. In certain relationships you may not have a strong need for affection, but in others you will. Some people have a greater need for control in their relationships, while others would rather follow a leader. When we have greater awareness of our interpersonal needs and the needs of the people we associate with, it's easier to meet their expectations and ensure our own needs are fulfilled as well.

Interpersonal skills for an intercultural world

An additional challenge to understanding interpersonal needs is knowing the expectations of people from different countries and cultures. Our world is getting smaller and smaller, and we are coming into contact with people from different places on a more regular basis. It could be that you travel a lot with your work, or maybe you speak with clients and colleagues in other countries. You could even be living in the same town you grew up in and are beginning to notice an influx of new people from foreign lands. Or maybe you get your international fix over the Internet, e-mailing and chatting with friends far away.

Whatever your situation, when coming into contact with people from other cultures, you will be confronted with beliefs and ways of doing things that you might not be accustomed to. You need to learn how to respond to them appropriately. Cross-cultural awareness is essential in our global community. Throughout the pages of this book you will find tips on how to apply people skills in an international setting, and points you may need to watch out for.

People skills in practice

Many of the skills and techniques discussed in this book will not be new to you. We know that we should listen actively, speak respectfully and honour our relationships, don't we? Yet still, when we put our interpersonal skills into practice, we don't always do what we know we should. When we are emotionally charged it can be hard not to get defensive or unintentionally say something hurtful.

My challenge for you as you read this book is to take a long, hard look at yourself and become more aware of your actions and reactions. Don't just read, learn. And don't just learn, practise. You will develop stronger, healthier and longer-lasting relationships as a result.

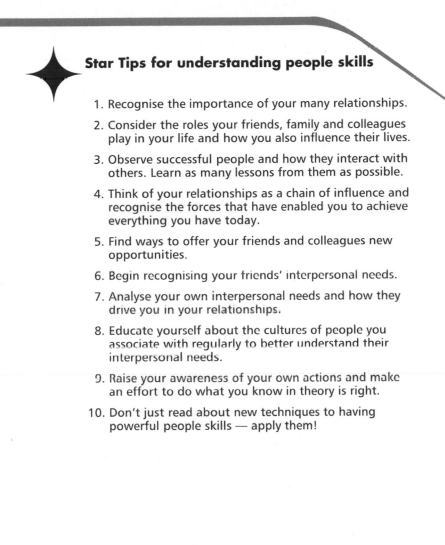

Star Tips for understanding people skills

1. Recognise the importance of your many relationships.

2. Consider the roles your friends, family and colleagues play in your life and how you also influence their lives.

3. Observe successful people and how they interact with others. Learn as many lessons from them as possible.

4. Think of your relationships as a chain of influence and recognise the forces that have enabled you to achieve everything you have today.

5. Find ways to offer your friends and colleagues new opportunities.

6. Begin recognising your friends' interpersonal needs.

7. Analyse your own interpersonal needs and how they drive you in your relationships.

8. Educate yourself about the cultures of people you associate with regularly to better understand their interpersonal needs.

9. Raise your awareness of your own actions and make an effort to do what you know in theory is right.

10. Don't just read about new techniques to having powerful people skills — apply them!

PREPARING FOR NEW RELATIONSHIPS

"Too often we underestimate the power of a touch, a smile, a kind word, a listening ear, an honest compliment, or the smallest act of caring, all of which have the potential to turn a life around."

Leo Buscaglia

Do you dread meeting new people? Does the invitation to a business networking event, a big company social or a distant friend's wedding immediately spark a frantic brainstorm of the most believable excuses to get out of attending? It isn't always easy meeting new people, but how much do you do to prepare for new encounters? It's just as important to prepare yourself for new relationships as it is to prepare for a job interview, an important presentation or a meeting with your staff.

The key to developing powerful people skills and approaching new relationships with the right attitude is, first and foremost, to take a long, hard look at yourself, your values and the assumptions that drive your own actions and reactions to the people you meet. Once you have a better understanding of yourself, you will be better prepared to embark on new relationships with others. In this chapter, I will help you to do just that — take a look at yourself from the inside out.

Becoming self-aware

What do you value most in your life? What beliefs have been engrained in you and what are your expectations of others? These questions are important because their answers act as the lens through which you view the world. People who have high self-awareness are more capable of understanding how their own values and beliefs influence their judgements of, and interactions with, others.

But becoming self-aware can be challenging. Things always seem clearer when looking from the outside in. It's easy to find fault in others and notice what they could change to become better people, but when it comes to taking a look at ourselves, our view becomes a bit distorted. Sometimes we don't realise when we are dominating conversations, saying insensitive things or judging others without reason.

So what steps can we take to achieve self-awareness? You need to have what I describe in my workshops as regular 'out-of-body' experiences. This means taking every opportunity to view yourself from the perspective of other people. When you are in meetings, on the telephone, at networking events, or even at a friend's dinner party, ask yourself whether you would enjoy speaking with you, doing business with you, or would be interested in getting to know you better. You may be surprised by your answers.

 Try This

Challenge yourself to have more 'out-of-body' experiences. It can be difficult to look at yourself objectively, so it may help to ask a trusted friend for feedback on your behaviour. Be prepared to accept that feedback, and try your hardest to understand it. Do not take what your friend says personally, although this is a very personal subject. Remember that it's easier to see things from the outside in, and if your friend has noticed a certain type of behaviour, chances are other people will have recognised it as well. Use the opportunity to make some positive changes to your behaviour.

When you begin to take an honest look at who you are and what drives you in your relationships with others, it is possible you will find certain areas that could use attention. Perhaps you dominate conversations and could work on your listening skills. Your body language may make you seem arrogant or aloof and you hadn't realised it. Maybe your nervousness around new people causes you to clam up and not say a single word, and as a result, you seem uninterested and disconnected from others.

Fast Fact

Even if you learn and understand every concept outlined in this book, you will not have more successful relationships until you have a better understanding of how you really act and how others really view you.

What categorising others says about you

Another way that you can learn more about yourself and how you view the world is by taking a look at how you categorise the people around you. When we meet people, we can't help but make judgements about them. That's just what humans do. We like to put people into categories that make sense to us personally. Depending on where you are in your life, your categories may change as the things that are important to you change.

For example, before I had a baby, I took little notice as to whether other people had children because it made no difference to me. Now that I have a child, I more consciously place those with children into the 'parent' category because it is one more thing I have in common with them. I can turn to that category of people for help, support and parenting advice when needed, because I know they will understand what I'm going through. Additionally, I might have more patience with these people because I have a better understanding of the added responsibilities and commitments they have to their families.

Whether or not this category I've created is appropriate or fair doesn't really matter. What is important is that I am aware of the fact that a 'parent' category exists. It says something about my values and priorities and definitely affects how I interact with people — with both positive and negative consequences.

Try This

You have already sub-consciously categorised the people you know. Write down those categories. Be honest with yourself. Maybe you distinguish between business owners and employees, locals and foreigners, young and old, tall and short, rich and poor, or any number of other categories. Some people you know will fall into several different categories. None of this matters as much as the actual categories you choose.

Take a look at your categories and ask what they say about you and the way you interact with people. Why is it important to you if people are married, single or divorced? Do you treat people in different categories differently? Why?

Facing your stereotypes

In my workshops on interpersonal skills, I break the participants into small groups and give each group a picture of a person. I then ask them to make a list of everything they feel they can determine about that person based on the picture alone. What the groups don't know is that they have all received pictures of the same person — a female model posing in all different types of clothing and situations. In one picture she's wearing a power suit and carrying a briefcase, in another she is picking out fruit with a young girl in a market, and in a third picture she's running on the beach with a dog. Each group comes up with very different stories about the woman based on her picture. And their assumptions say a lot about the values and beliefs that drive them.

I've heard some very interesting responses. The woman with the child is married. Why? Because she must be married if she has a small child! The woman running on the beach works freelance. Who else has the time to take runs on the beach? And she must be an animal lover since she has a dog. The successful business woman is definitely married because, well, she's just too old to be single, and would she really buy that jewellery for herself?

As shocking as some of these answers may seem, they provide amazing insights about the driving forces behind the participants' values and belief systems. When they realise all the pictures are of the same woman doing different things, it becomes obvious how powerful stereotypes can be.

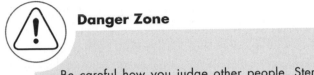

Danger Zone

Be careful how you judge other people. Stereotypes are powerful, and they are hard to change once we've made our minds up.

It's all about attitude

When you are faced with an opportunity to meet new people, your attitude will have a lot to do with the success of that encounter. If you enter new relationships with an open mind and positive outlook, not only are you going to seem more friendly, approachable and trustworthy, you will also be presenting your best self. If, on the other hand, you have feelings of self-doubt and disinterest in engaging new people, your attitude will most likely create a self-fulfilling prophecy. The people you meet will not be drawn to you, and they will recognise the same insecurities that you have been focusing on.

Aha! Moment

The law of attraction is at work in my relationships. I will attract what I put at the forefront of my mind. If I'm positive, other positive people will be drawn to me.

Myth Buster

It doesn't matter what I do or say, because I do not have any control over the outcome of social interactions or whether people like me.

This could not be farther from the truth. People who live by this assumption allow other people to determine the course of their interactions. They take a passive approach to their relationships, and believe that the problem always lies elsewhere and not with them. Unless you take responsibility for your actions and interactions, you will never be able to form long-lasting, meaningful relationships.

Your attitude is up to you. You may not realise it, but your attitude is a choice. You can choose positivity just as easily as you can choose negativity. When interacting with others, some attitudes will get you nowhere. Jealousy, anger, impatience, vengefulness, embarrassment and disrespectfulness are all examples of really bad attitudes in social and professional interactions. Instead, you can choose to be supportive, enthusiastic, confident, patient, welcoming, helpful or engaging.

Five factors that can negatively affect your attitude

1. Lack of sleep

It's tough to present yourself well and have a good attitude when you're sleep-deprived. Make sure you get at least 7–8 hours of rest each night so that you look and feel fresh, energised and approachable.

2. Stress

Stress can be extremely detrimental to maintaining a positive attitude. Find ways to reduce stress in your life so that you don't accidentally take it out on other people. This is one of the worst results of a stressful lifestyle, and it does nothing to help you build and maintain strong relationships.

3. Private problems

Sometimes you might just be having a bad day, and when it rains, it pours! If you're having one of these days, remember not to dump your negativity on the people around you. Soak up their positivity instead!

4. Emotional sensitivities

Try to remain emotionally neutral in your dealings with other people. If you let your emotions get the best of you, your attitude will suffer immediately, and you could end up regretting an inappropriate reaction to something another person says or does.

5. Poor self-esteem

If you're battling your own insecurities, it's extremely difficult to maintain a positive attitude. Poor self-esteem is the number one reason people lack confidence in meeting new people or sustaining already established relationships.

 Aha! Moment

It's up to me to choose a positive attitude and prepare myself mentally and emotionally for new relationships.

Building your confidence and self-esteem

Even when people know what they need to do to create more successful relationships, they often lack the confidence to put their plans into action. Self-esteem and self-confidence are very closely related. Low self-esteem will directly affect your attitude (as we learnt in the last section), and it can completely erode your relationships. It will pay dividends in all areas of your life if you actively work on improving your self-esteem.

People with healthy self-esteem:

- consider themselves worthy of being loved and loving others.

- have an optimistic outlook on life and are excited about the future.

- are able to accept responsibility for their actions.

- perceive themselves the same way as they project themselves to others.

- have effective coping strategies and are able to keep their problems in perspective.

- are productive and active in achieving their goals.

- believe they deserve good things.

- do not feel the need to compare themselves to others.

- are satisfied with their lives, their surroundings and their relationships.

If you find that you are lacking any of these qualities, it may be time to actively work on improving the way you feel about yourself. Yes, this is a lot easier said than done, but here are seven steps you can take to actively increase your confidence and prepare yourself for new relationships:

1. Remind yourself that nobody's perfect

Everyone makes mistakes and no one expects perfection. Once you have more realistic expectations for yourself, you do not need to be so nervous in new situations.

2. Don't take yourself too seriously

Enjoy your life and the people you share it with. Learn to laugh at yourself and your faults.

3. Focus on the positives instead of the negatives in your life

There is always a silver lining — even in the most negative situations.

4. Put your problems in perspective

Where do your problems really rank when compared to the ills of the world?

5. Keep a journal

This is an excellent way to relieve yourself of your negative thoughts and feelings. Once you've written them down, let them go. You no longer need to dwell on these negative aspects of your life. Better yet, keep a gratitude journal where you only focus on the positive things that you are grateful for. When you remind yourself how much you have, you suddenly won't be as bothered by what you don't.

6. Get some exercise

The endorphins created will give you increased energy, plus you'll also start feeling better about the way you look and feel.

7. Re-acquaint yourself with old friends

Individuals with low self-esteem tend to fracture relationships and push people out of their lives. Get back in touch with old friends and re-enter your old social scenes (or new ones) to feel re-connected with others.

 Aha! Moment

By harbouring negative feelings about myself I am sabotaging my relationships with others. It is important that I learn to be comfortable with myself so that I can become more comfortable around other people. When I feel good about myself, other people will notice and will be drawn to my confidence and positive outlook on life.

Fighting your nerves

Even with a healthy dose of self-esteem, many of us get nervous about meeting new people. Our nervousness is usually directly related to how much is riding on the meeting. Think about it. Will you be more nervous in an interview for the job you want most, or the job you'd rather not get?

A good friend of mine was recently set up on a blind date. She was incredibly nervous beforehand, because maybe, just maybe, this man was the man of her dreams. When she finally met him, she was still very nervous, but after about 10 minutes of talking to him, she could see that this was not going to be a love connection. Suddenly her nervousness faded. When she was no longer emotionally involved in the encounter, she was able to relax and enjoy the rest of her evening for what it was worth. After all, they may not have been fated to be together, but that doesn't mean they couldn't become friends.

And therein lies the secret to controlling our nerves: by keeping our emotions separate from our experiences, we are able to maintain better control. When you aren't emotionally attached to a possible job offer, it's a lot easier to get through the interview. When you aren't interested in someone romantically, it's a lot easier to just have a nice time and not worry about what will come of the encounter. Wouldn't it be great if we were able to approach all new situations in this way?

Getting your image in order

Self-confidence and self-esteem go a long way in helping you present yourself well, but you'll be pleased to hear that there are even easier ways to get your image in order. It would be worth taking some time to think about the image you currently project and whether or not it is in line with your personal and professional goals. This is another instance where feedback from trusted friends can be very useful.

Here are three easy ways you can improve your image:

1. Smile

Everyone loves a smiling face. This is the single most effective action you can take to become more approachable, appear more confident and draw more positive people into your life.

2. Have good posture

Correct posture not only makes you look more confident, but it will actually help you feel more confident too. We'll talk about the specific steps you can take to improve your posture in Chapter 5.

3. Dress appropriately

Wear clean and neat clothes that present a professional image and are appropriate for your profession or event.

Danger Zone

When choosing your style of dress for an event, avoid anything too informal. You can never ruin your reputation by being too formal, but you can lose standing by showing up for a formal event dressed inappropriately.

Myth Buster

By consciously changing my image and the way I present myself to others, I am not being honest or authentic in my dealings with them.

I have also questioned this point before, but have come to realise that we all have many different faces. When I hang around the house on a Saturday afternoon, I look nothing like the professional speaker and trainer that my clients see. Am I being hypocritical by not showing up to meetings in my favourite t-shirt and shorts? Absolutely not. I'm consciously presenting my best self and the side of me that is most appropriate for the situation.

Getting out there

The best way to overcome your fears and insecurities is to simply get out there and start meeting new people. This chapter has given you the foundation to prepare yourself for new relationships. The rest of this book will give you the specific tools to use when you find yourself in various interpersonal situations. The only way to improve any skill is to practise, practise, practise.

If going out to meet new people is too big of a jump for you, then start by re-committing yourself to your current relationships. Have more 'out-of-body' experiences, and study how you are currently interacting with others. Are you being the best friend, colleague or partner you can be?

★ Star Tips for preparing yourself for new relationships

1. Become more aware of your values and beliefs when interacting with others.

2. Think about how you categorise people and what those categories say about you.

3. Face your stereotypes and commit yourself to giving everyone a fair and equal chance. Get to know people before you try to judge them.

4. Choose to have a positive attitude and don't misdirect your stress and grief towards others.

5. Remember that you do have choices and can control the course of your interactions.

6. Work on your self-esteem so that you can give yourself fully to your relationships.

7. Control your nerves by separating your emotions from your encounters with others.

8. Present a professional and confident image by dressing well and putting your best face forward.

9. Prepare yourself mentally and emotionally to meet new people.

10. Get out there and put your new skills to the test!

HOW TO CLICK FROM
THE MOMENT YOU MEET

*"Lust is easy. Love is hard.
Like is most important."*

Carl Reiner

3

There is nothing better than the natural high that comes from really connecting with someone new. When you find yourself in a new company or a new town, where you don't know anyone or have any friends, you quickly realise the power of connecting with others. Meeting someone new and feeling like you had some rapport with them can make your day, give you renewed energy and make you feel like you belong to something larger than yourself.

Rapport isn't always easy to build. We don't always click with people the first time we meet (or the second or third time). In this chapter we'll be taking a look at the keys to building rapport and useful techniques you can use to better establish it from the start.

Showing your authentic self

My favourite word in the English language is 'authenticity'. For me, it means, 'what you see is what you get'. It means that I am me, and you are you, and we both are real, living, breathing people sharing our true selves with each other. People who are not authentic do not last long in my circles, and if they do hang around, they'll never end up being very close friends. I give my honest self to my relationships, and if I don't feel as though I'm getting that in return, I find it challenging to maintain an open, honest friendship.

The same is true in business. I won't work with anyone I don't trust, and I definitely don't want to buy anything or invest in anyone I don't feel comfortable with. If a salesman doesn't seem authentic to me, I question his character. If a service provider seems too eager to impress, I question her credentials.

Fast Fact

Merriam-Webster's Online Dictionary defines *authentic* as "true to one's own personality, spirit or character".

In high school, I struggled, like most teens, to find myself and fit in. In college, I did and said things that, looking back, make me wonder what I was possibly thinking at the time. As an adult, I've worked in companies where I've tried to change myself to fit their culture — without success. I've learnt that when I'm not true to myself, I'm not truly happy. I've also learnt that when I'm not happy, I have a hard time making other people happy.

I'm so grateful to have learnt this lesson at a relatively young age without spending 20 years doing something that I know, deep down, isn't right for me. I've unfortunately heard too many stories like this, and know too many people who are unhappily living this way.

I have two acquaintances who serve as good examples of people who are not being true to their own character. I have known them both for quite some time now and we've had several conversations, yet I still don't feel like I know who either one of them truly is. They both have similar habits. Their speech is methodical — almost rehearsed — and their tone is drawn out as if I should hang on every word. Their vocabulary is unnatural and makes me think they spend their nights reading thesauruses. Their gestures are stiff and robotic and sometimes I wonder if they were taken directly out of a public speaking textbook.

The problem is that there is a mismatch. Their words, tone and actions just don't seem to fit. Something is out of place — and when you're being authentic, nothing is out of place. Your messages naturally and seamlessly complement your being.

Imagine how hard it must be for unauthentic people to put on a façade each and every day. It must take so much time and energy to pretend to be someone they are not. And think how low their self-esteem must be if they really think these actions are necessary!

Authenticity is all about being comfortable in your own skin — with who you are as a person underneath it all. When you are being authentic, you aren't trying to impress, amaze or enchant those around you. You are simply putting your vulnerable self out there and saying, "Here I am world. Take me or leave me." And this is precisely what can be so scary for many people. "What if people choose to leave me?" the insecure person asks himself. The confident person doesn't even stop to think about such things.

 Fast Fact

Authentic people attract the masses. They are well-known and well-liked. They are not only comfortable with themselves, but somehow, they make you feel more comfortable too. You will know instinctively if someone is authentic because you will feel good around that person. If you have a 'funny feeling' about someone, it is most likely because she is hiding a part of herself from you.

True authenticity is achieved when all the messages you send are in sync. Verbally, the words you use are simple and natural. Vocally, you sound relaxed, and your pitch, resonance, volume, pace and intonation fit both you and the situation. Visually, your gestures and movements are unforced and emphasise your points. As a package, the verbal, vocal and visual elements just fit. We'll go into further detail about these three areas and how they work in the next three chapters, but for now, just be aware of how they fit together to define who you are and the image you project.

 Aha! Moment

To live a happier life, and make more friends in the process, all I have to do is be myself.

Self-disclosure — how much is too much?

Being authentic does not mean you have to lay it all out on the table the first time you meet someone. We don't need to hear your entire life story or be bombarded with your very strong opinions on just about everything.

Meeting people for the first time is all about reading the situation, the people in it, and moderating your own behaviour to fit the crowd and setting. If you can do this, you will be more successful in building rapport and clicking with everyone you meet.

Myth Buster

When I meet new people, I need to say something really funny or shocking so they'll remember me.

Unless you're auditioning for a reality television show, tone down the dramatic outbursts. You'll find that disclosing shocking details about yourself will only make the people around you feel uncomfortable. They might remember you, but it will be for the wrong reasons.

Ten things I don't need to know about you when we meet

1. Anything related to your sexual activities, history or preferences.

2. Your philosophy as to how your problematic childhood has shaped you as a person.

3. The story of your most tragic life experience.

4. A list of your most fantastic awards, honours and achievements.

5. Your deepest darkest secret that I should be sure to keep confidential.

6. Your annual income, the size of your house or the kind of car you drive.

7. The most embarrassing thing that has ever happened to you.

8. Anything that has to do with your body and how it functions (or doesn't function).

9. The details of your most recent appointment with your psychiatrist.

10. A confession of the mortal sins you have committed throughout your life.

Danger Zone

When you're travelling in international circles, be even more careful about the information you choose to disclose to others. People from other cultures may be more conservative than you are. What might seem like 'no big deal' to you could be quite shocking to someone else. Use common sense and be tasteful and respectful.

I like you because you're like me

When you meet people for the first time, finding something to talk about to get the conversation going can be a bit like trying to find the end of a rainbow. You don't know where to begin or where the rainbow will lead. But in the end, there's a great reward — a pot of gold! Your energy, and level of interest in finding it, will determine whether you, and your new acquaintance, will benefit from its wealth.

Once you find your pot of gold, all the awkwardness of a first encounter disappears. This is because the pot of gold contains all the common interests you share with the other person. Pick up just one gold coin and you'll be able to talk openly and naturally for hours!

Here are some commonalities you might find in your pot of gold:

- you come from the same town.

- you went to the same school (at the same or different times).

- you know the same people.

- you live (or lived) in the same neighbourhood.

- you have the same hobbies.

- you play the same sports.

- you work in the same company or industry.

Aha! Moment

I'll have a better chance of connecting with new people if I try to find out more about them and the things we may have in common.

Try This

Think about some of the most important relationships in your life right now. What pots of gold do you share with each person? If you have an important relationship in your life with someone who you don't seem to click with, what possible pot of gold could you be missing? Is there anything you can do to enhance your relationship with that person?

Fast Fact

Just as you won't like everyone you meet, not everyone is going to like you. That's normal, and it's okay. You could do everything right — be confident, smile, have a positive attitude and be a gifted conversationalist. Still, there will be people who don't like you. You don't have to click with everyone. It would be unnatural if you did. Don't dwell on it or take it personally. Just move on.

If the person happens to be someone you need to associate with on a regular basis, such as a co-worker or boss, recognise your differences and respect them for what they are. You can have very fulfilling relationships with people who are different than you if you honour your different opinions, ways of thinking and outlooks on life.

Taking a sincere interest in others

You can still build rapport with someone, even if you're having trouble finding something in common. The key is to take a sincere interest in that person. Dale Carnegie wrote, "Remember that the people you are talking to are a hundred times more interested in themselves and their wants and problems than they are in you and your problems." Try to find something interesting in every person you meet and make a sincere effort to learn more about them.

By getting other people to talk about their own 'wants and problems' you give them an outlet to share things about themselves and connect with you.

 Danger Zone

There is a big difference between showing interest in what a person is saying and interrogating a person. Read Chapters 4 to 7 carefully to learn different ways of showing interest with active listening techniques, visual and vocal cues, and asking the right kinds of questions that allow people to open up without feeling uncomfortable.

Have you ever noticed that the people who say the least in conversations are usually considered to be the best conversationalists and are the most liked by others? I learnt this lesson the hard way. I met a lady named Christina at a conference and we had a fantastic conversation. I told a good friend about this wonderful woman I met. She was so nice, friendly and funny. My friend asked me what she did for a living. Hmm… I wasn't sure. Where was she from? I didn't know that either. Was she married? Did she have any children? I had no idea. Finally my friend said, "So basically, you met a lady named Christina, you know nothing about her, but she's one of the most fantastic people you've ever met?"

How could that be? I replayed our conversation in my mind. I really felt like we had connected. I must have learnt something about her! I was so embarrassed when I realised I hadn't learnt one single thing beyond her name. This woman had taken what seemed to me to be a sincere interest in every single little thing I said. I dominated the entire conversation without even realising it. I couldn't believe it. I wanted to rewind the tape and start over, but it was far too late. I thought she was fantastic, but I wonder what she thought of me. What an important lesson I learnt!

Myth Buster

If people are going to get to know me and like me, then surely I need to talk a lot.

On the contrary! To be well-liked, you don't always have to be the one doing the talking. By taking a sincere interest in others, you can make them feel good about themselves, comfortable with the situation and more importantly, comfortable with you!

Try This

Next time you meet someone new, think about how much information you are sharing as compared to the other person. Make it your goal to let the other person speak at least 60 per cent of the time. Take a sincere interest in what he has to say, and you'll find that he will open up more and more as your signs of interest give him permission to do so.

Using empathy effectively

If you have empathy, you are able to put yourself in another person's shoes mentally and emotionally. You understand what the other person is experiencing so well that you think their thoughts and feel their emotions as if they were your own. People who are masters of empathy will connect with just about anyone and make friends everywhere. The reason for this is that, as we learnt in Chapter 1, one of our deepest desires and interpersonal needs is inclusion. We want to feel like we're part of something larger than ourselves. We don't feel so alone when we meet other people who feel the same way about something as we do. We feel accepted when people say, "I understand how you feel."

The first step to being able to show empathy is to be aware of the mood around you. When you enter a conversation, the people talking could be loudly joking about a funny experience they shared, or they could be speaking in hushed tones and comforting one another. Your job is to read the mood by carefully studying the body language, tone and words of the speaker and those around him. You need to be able to match a person's emotional state and then respond accordingly.

Empathy is just as important in business as it is in our personal relationships. If you can't connect with your customer or client on an emotional level, you will never be able to sell your product or service well. You need to be able to understand (emotionally) the customer need that your product fulfils. Most of our purchases are emotionally driven, so if you can tap into those feelings, you will be much more successful.

For example, John and Linda recently had a baby boy and know that it's important to start saving for his future education. They go to Frank, the financial advisor, to ask him what he thinks they should do. Frank focuses on the numbers and shows them how rich he can make them if they invest in his financial products. The numbers look reasonable, but John and Linda just don't get a good feeling from Frank. He's so focused on their financial needs that he forgets to attend to their emotional ones. They decide to get a second opinion.

They call their friend's advisor, Dru, and set up a meeting. Before they even begin discussing their finances, Dru congratulates them on the birth of their baby boy and shares in their excitement about being new parents. He asks them how they're feeling and whether they've been getting any sleep. He tells them what a wonderful decision they've made to invest in their son's future so early on and that they are already proving to be good parents. Dru tells them their son is very lucky to have parents like them.

John and Linda are pleased after meeting with Dru and choose to invest with him. His products weren't much different from Frank's, but they felt like they clicked with Dru and were more comfortable doing business with him. He seemed to understand what it was like to be a new parent. He was able to empathise with them and share in their dream of a secure future for their son.

Relationships have their beginnings in the very first few seconds you meet someone. Whether or not you click will determine the course of that relationship beyond your first meeting. Show your authentic self and uncover the common interests you share with people. If you take a sincere interest in their needs and connect with them on an emotional level, you'll be more likely to build long-lasting relationships.

Star Tips for building rapport and connecting with people

1. Be true to yourself. You will win more friends and make stronger connections with people by being authentic.

2. Don't try to impress, enchant or amaze — by engaging in open, honest conversation, you'll achieve this objective anyway.

3. Choose the information you disclose about yourself during a first meeting wisely.

4. Use some energy to discover the 'pot of gold' that you share with others.

5. Take a sincere interest in other people and their interests.

6. Allow other people to talk more than you do and pay attention to what they say.

7. Always tell the truth. Even the smallest lie or exaggeration could ruin a relationship.

8. Have respect for other people's opinions and ideas.

9. Send one synchronised, authentic message visually, verbally and vocally.

10. Moderate your behaviour to fit the people and situation you find yourself in.

LISTENING
TO UNDERSTAND

"A good listener is not only popular everywhere, but after a while he gets to know something."

Wilson Mizner

4

When you are focused on building and maintaining strong relationships, listening is the most important interpersonal skill to master. So much more than merely hearing what a person is saying, listening has to do with truly understanding what someone is saying and feeling — without letting your own judgements, opinions and solutions take over the conversation.

Listening gone wrong

Have you ever had a conversation with someone and felt that everything you said went in one ear and out the other? Or have you ever noticed yourself suddenly 'zoning out' and missing part (or all) of what someone has said? These are perfect examples of communication failures on the part of the listener.

What exactly is going wrong in our conversations that forces us to repeat ourselves time and time again, explain what we really mean and fight for the attention of our listeners? Usually it's not so much what we're saying but how the listener is, or more likely isn't, listening.

Here are four of the most common listening pitfalls. Do you ever notice yourself making one of these mistakes?

1. Making judgements

I call this the 'I'm right, you're wrong' mentality. Instead of opening your mind to really understand what someone is saying and their point of view, you are instead trying to decide whether or not you agree with what the person is saying while they are saying it. The problem here is that while you're busy deciding your position on each of their points, you're missing the subtleties of their argument that make all the difference in their meaning. If you listen to understand, instead of to judge, you might find that you have more in common with the speaker than you think.

Danger Zone

The most common roadblock to active listening is making judgements about what you think the speaker is trying to say.

In order to understand where a person is coming from, it is important that you keep an open mind and don't let your own thoughts and assumptions colour the message the speaker is trying to get across.

2. Finishing the other person's thoughts

Do you and your partner finish each other's sentences? This trait is usually seen as being a good thing. We feel like we click with each other when we think and say the same things at the same time. Sometimes though, what you're thinking might not be what the speaker is saying, and your interruptions may hurt more than help. When you make assumptions about where someone is going with their ideas, opinions or stories, you run the risk of breaking rapport instead of building it.

3. Solving the speaker's problem

Imagine that your friend, Anne, begins telling you about a problem she's having with her boss, husband, best friend, colleague, employee, child's teacher or someone else. Do you really listen to what Anne is saying and feeling, or are you trying to think of some advice you can give or a way to solve her problem? Sometimes people aren't looking for solutions. They're just looking for a good friend to listen and empathise.

 Aha! Moment

Not everyone wants their problems *solved*. Often people just want someone to *listen*. It's best if I stop trying to fix everything, and just be a friend!

4. Letting your emotions get the best of you

When you listen to what someone is saying, your goal should always be to understand what the person is thinking and feeling. Try not to let your thoughts and emotions get in the way of understanding what the speaker is trying to say. If you feel your emotions bubbling up to the surface, take a deep breath and refocus on the speaker's message. You'll have plenty of time to process your own thoughts and feelings later. First, make sure you get the message straight.

Danger Zone

Keep your emotions in check. When you are listening to someone, try not to react emotionally to what is being said. Your emotions can blind you to what the speaker is actually saying. It's very possible that you are overreacting and the situation is not as terrible as you think. Do your best to understand what is really being said, and don't let your emotions get the best of you.

It doesn't really matter which bad listening habit you have, the result is the same — instead of listening to understand, you are gearing the conversation and your own thoughts back to yourself and your concerns instead of the speaker and his concerns.

When you pass judgement, try to finish the speaker's thoughts or solve all their problems, you're focusing on what you think is important instead of paying attention to the speaker's needs, feelings and desires. You could also end up missing out on some truly important information that the speaker never got the chance to reveal. Instead of focusing on ourselves, we need to focus on others.

Try This

Before entering an important meeting, an interview or even a cocktail party, clear your mind of clutter and focus your energy on the people around you. If you are thinking about the e-mail you just read, the meeting you had that afternoon or are preoccupied with the fact that you're having a bad hair day, you're not going to be doing what's most important — listening.

Listening to what isn't being said

Sometimes the most important parts of our messages aren't actually spoken. To be an effective listener, you will need to learn to listen with all of your senses.

Watch the speaker.

Listen to the speaker's words.

Feel the emotions in the speaker's voice.

Fast Fact

Over 90 per cent of our messages are sent non-verbally through body language and tone of voice. Your friend, John, might say he's "doing great", but does he really mean it?

Active listening requires that you look at the person who is speaking. This means closing your laptop, putting down your magazine, or whatever latest gadget you're addicted to, and looking the person in their eyes as they speak.

Although this is common sense, it's easier said than done. I don't know how many times my husband, Peter, has had to repeat what he just said because I was determined to multi-task. I like to think I'm good at checking my e-mail and listening to him at the same time, but unfortunately I'm not! I hear the first three words of what he says and then suddenly, the silence when he's finished. I've learnt that I have to actually close my laptop and turn my chair to face him when he speaks. Otherwise, I can't be trusted to listen fully!

It's also important to face the person speaking so that you can read their body language. We'll go into greater detail in the next chapter, but some of the most important things to notice are the speaker's eye contact (or lack of it), posture and gestures. Is there something about your friend Lisa's posture that reveals she might not be as happy as she seems? Does your colleague, Craig, avoid making eye contact when giving you the latest sales figures? Could he be hiding something or be nervous to tell you more?

 Aha! Moment

Body language doesn't lie. If I read the signals being sent, I can gain greater insight into what a person is thinking and feeling.

Although just a small percentage of a person's message is encoded in the words used, it is still important to listen to what is (and isn't) being said. Some people will always say it like it is with honesty and authenticity. These are the people I like to spend my time with. Unfortunately, they are few and far between.

More often than not we need to read into what people say to find their true meaning. Some people will say they are "fine" simply because they don't want to talk about how awful they really feel, or they don't want to boast about how fantastic their lives are!

Emotions are incredibly hard for a lot of people to talk about. It takes a good listener to help others open up and feel comfortable. If you are committed to listening without passing judgement, you will find that more people choose to open up to you. This, of course, is only true if you are also the type of person that can be trusted.

Communicating that you're listening

Cicero wrote that "silence is one of the great arts of conversation", but for many of us, silence has become awkward. We hold onto the crazy notion that for a conversation to be successful there can't be any pauses or lulls. But without silence, when do we have time to absorb what has been said? And when does the speaker have time to think about what to say next?

One way to communicate that you are listening is to allow for what's been called 'attentive silence'. Sometimes speakers need a few more seconds to finish their thoughts. If they break eye contact and become silent, it usually means they are thinking about what to say next. Don't jump in with your response yet. When they wrap up their comments and look you in the eyes, it is a sign that they are finished and it's your turn to speak.

Here are a few ways you can signal with your body language that you are listening attentively during a conversation:

- Lean slightly towards the speaker

- Nod your head

- Hold eye contact

- Smile (or frown if appropriate)

- Sit or stand up straight

It goes without saying that negative body language like yawning, slumping down in your chair or perching your head up on your hands are not the best signals to send someone you care about.

Fast Fact

Your body language is linked with your emotions and state of being. Attentive body language, like leaning forward, will also influence your mental state and help you to focus better on what a person is saying.

Don't forget the subtle verbal cues you can send to show that you're listening. Lightly sprinkled throughout the conversation, these short responses are important signals to the speaker that you're following what they are saying.

"Uh-huh..."

"Wow!"

"Really?"

"Hmmm..."

"I see..."

"Oh..."

From listening to collaborating

Of course a conversation wouldn't be a conversation if you only sat there listening and occasionally added a thoughtful, *"Mm-hmm..."* At some point you are going to have to answer! But how can you answer in an appropriate way that carries the conversation forward, doesn't make the other person uncomfortable and shows that you have understood the speaker's message?

Your brilliant responses in conversations should meet at least one of the following criteria. They should:

- clarify what has been said.

  "So what you're saying is…"

  "Have I understood you correctly? You mean…"

- relate to the speaker on an emotional level.

  "I would feel the same way…"

  "I know you feel disappointed by her actions…"

 Aha! Moment

Emotions are very difficult for many people to verbalise, but if I can understand and reflect how a person is feeling, I will find that I am able to make a more powerful and meaningful connection with that person.

- help the speaker tell his story by emphasising what has been said.

When you emphasise a certain point the speaker has made, you give him permission to elaborate on that point. Your goal should be to increase your understanding of the speaker's story and help the speaker tell their story in a more detailed fashion. Let's look at two examples:

#1   Jeffrey: It was a long meeting, and everyone seemed happy with the decisions that were made.

     You: **Seemed** *happy?*

#2   Amanda: He said they didn't like the show.

     You: **Didn't** *like it? Why not?*

Some inappropriate responses are ones that:

- **are tasteless or untimely.**

  In the television series *Friends*, the character, Chandler, has the bad habit of doing or saying really foolish things when his friends most need him to listen and be there for them. He thinks that he is lightening the mood but he is actually just trying to escape what, to him, is an uncomfortable situation. Ironically, he usually ends up making the situation even more uncomfortable for everyone.

  Don't try to crack jokes or change the subject simply so you can feel more comfortable. It's disrespectful to the speaker and only serves to devalue their feelings.

- **involve multiple questions.**

  No one likes to feel like they're on trial. It's okay to ask the occasional question, especially if you are asking for clarification, but grilling the speaker with a list of questions can make you seem nosey, or worse, obsessed.

Myth Buster

Asking lots of questions shows you're listening.

Not necessarily. When people are trying to be 'active listeners' one of the first mistakes they make is to ask too many questions. Most of the questions end up relating to the listener's concerns instead of the speaker's. Also, the speaker begins to feel more and more uncomfortable as the listener continues to grill for information.

- turn into long-winded tangential stories.

I always thought that sharing a similar story of my own was a good way to connect with a speaker until I met a woman who did this all the time. I talked about my cat and she had a friend who had the same type of cat. I told her about my friend getting married and she told me about the five weddings she had attended that year. I told her about a trip I took in Asia and she told me all the details of her sister's trip to Cambodia.

It became so ridiculous that I actually tried to come up with the most extreme and random things to say just to challenge her to find a story that could somehow relate. She was incredibly gifted in this area! I eventually gave up. The bottom line was that I don't think she really heard a thing I said. Whenever I was talking she was searching the depths of her memory for a story on a similar topic. I felt no connection to her whatsoever and thought she was quite the know-it-all.

Myth Buster

Sharing a similar experience you've had will show the listener that you relate to him and understand what he's going through.

Sharing similar stories and experiences usually just brings the focus back to you, sending the signal that you are self-absorbed and not really listening to the speaker's concerns.

Listening on the phone

Listening skills become even more important when we take away visual cues and are forced to focus on only the voice and words of a speaker through the telephone. Despite all of our technological advances, the telephone still plays an incredibly important role in business. It's become common to take part in conference calls across borders and time zones. These types of calls pose additional challenges as you not only have to focus on what is being said, but you also need to sift through different accents and cultural norms to get to the point of the matter.

All the listening skills we've discussed in this chapter will help you on the phone, but here are some additional tools to employ during important calls.

- Take notes. When you hang up the phone you'll need to remember the important points that you discussed. You won't have the visual memory of seeing your caller tell you the information, nor will you have a written record — other than your notes.

- Double check that you've understood names, numbers and other important information correctly.

- Politely ask people to slow down if they're speaking too quickly.

- Let a caller know if you have a bad connection or are having trouble hearing them.

- Paraphrase points regularly to be sure that you've understood what has been said.

Becoming an active listener

Most people think they are good listeners. The majority of bosses would tell you that they always listen to the concerns of their employees and that they have a good understanding of how the people around them feel. Salespeople would say that they listen to their customers and know exactly what they need. Happy husbands and wives would share how they listen to and respect each other. But are you really *listening*?

Try This

Even if you think you're a good listener, take some time to observe yourself in action. Pay close attention to how you currently listen to people when you are having conversations. Ask yourself these questions:

- Do I interrupt the speaker often?

- Do I always have a similar story? Are my stories really relevant to what the speaker is saying?

- Do I allow for attentive silence or do I feel really uncomfortable?

- Do I give the speaker time to elaborate on her points?

- Do I read visual cues and know when I am expected to respond?

Be honest with yourself and make a list of the bad habits you would like to change. Return to this list regularly to record your progress.

By becoming more aware of what you are already doing right and what you might be doing wrong, you can begin to take steps towards changing your behaviour and improving your listening skills.

As we learnt in the last chapter, it is often easier to observe others than to observe ourselves. Pay attention to how other people react to you when you speak. In what ways do people make you feel more comfortable? When do you get the feeling that people aren't listening to you? How can you emulate the good listeners around you?

Listening skills must not be overlooked in your people skills toolkit. If you can master the art of truly listening to others, you will be able to connect with them in a more meaningful way. Listen with the goal of understanding, instead of trying to solve problems or judge what other people are trying to say. You'll find that your friends and colleagues will open up to you more and enjoy sharing their thoughts and feelings with you.

Star Tips for effective, active listening

1. Keep an open mind and do not pass judgement while listening.

2. Be a good friend and listen. You don't always have to solve everyone's problems.

3. Focus on the speaker and his concerns — not your own.

4. Listen to what isn't being said by paying attention to body language and questioning whether information is being omitted.

5. Control your emotional response to what is being said.

6. Use attentive body language to communicate that you're listening.

7. Make it your goal to understand what's being said, not judge it or try to finish the other person's thoughts.

8. Connect with the speaker emotionally by paying attention to visual and vocal cues.

9. Emphasise what a speaker says to help him tell his story more effectively.

10. Double-check for understanding, especially when you are on the telephone.

THE BENEFITS OF
BODY LANGUAGE

"Movement never lies. It is a barometer telling the state of the soul's weather."

Martha Graham

5

Every time you enter into a conversation with another person or group of people there are two simultaneous conversations going on — the verbal and the non-verbal. The verbal conversation is a conscious one, consisting of the words you use and how you use them. The non-verbal conversation is everything else, and is managed almost entirely by your sub-conscious mind. Your body and your voice combine to send more powerful messages than your words alone.

Are you aware of the messages you are really sending? And are you capable of decoding the messages that are being sent to your sub-conscious through other people's non-verbal behaviour? Let's take a closer look at this seemingly 'secret' code.

Understanding body language

Have you ever had a 'bad feeling' about someone? I'm sure you have. When we meet people for the first time, we actually decide right away whether we like them or not. Usually we have no idea what causes us to feel a certain way. It's just one of those 'gut feelings'. That feeling is actually your sub-conscious translating the non-verbal signals that are being sent to you by the other person. If something is out of alignment — for example, if the tone of voice or body language doesn't seem to match the verbal message being sent — you will suddenly feel confused. You end up feeling as though the person is hiding something from you. In reality he is. He's hiding his authentic self, and your sub-conscious has recognised it.

I always feel strange training people to study and understand body language because, assuming you have grown up around other humans, you are already a master of this language without even knowing it. You will find that you are surprisingly capable when it comes to understanding the visual signals that other people send. Take these faces for example. I'm willing to bet that you will have absolutely no problem deciphering the moods of these four people. If you doubt yourself, check your answers underneath.

(a)

(b)

(c)

(d)

Answers: (a) happy, (b) angry, (c) confused, (d) sad

So, how did you do? I'm sure it didn't take much guesswork to understand the messages these people were sending. If your best friend looked like person (d), but he told you he was feeling fine, what would you believe — the verbal or non-verbal message? We are so attuned to looking for the non-verbal message that it wins every time.

Try This

Find a crowded place like a park, an airport or a busy shopping centre, and just watch the people around you. When you see a couple or group, try to determine as much about them as you can. Are they good friends, colleagues, family members? Do they like each other? Are they in a fight? Did they make up again? You will be surprised how much of the situation you will be able to understand from a distance. What are the subtle clues that their body language sends?

Even though we are sub-consciously fluent in body language, we are still presented with some challenges. How many times has your first impression of someone been wrong? I have met many people who I feel I have misjudged in those first few minutes of conversation. I didn't like them at all when I first met them, but when we met again in a different setting, with different people and under different circumstances, suddenly we clicked. The opposite has also happened. I've really liked people the first time I met them but later discovered that they weren't at all how I had originally imagined. It's these times that I kick myself and think, "How did I not see that? How could I be so easily taken in by someone's charm that I failed to notice what was really underneath?"

Danger Zone

Be careful not to over-analyse or change your own body language too much. You run the risk of coming across as fake if your non-verbal message suddenly falls out of alignment with your verbal one.

Reading body signals and sending your own

It's very important that you are able to read other people's signals and also be aware of the sub-conscious signals you might be sending. When people think of body language, the first things they think of are gestures — the hand and body movements you make to illustrate your point. Although very important, gestures are only one small piece of the puzzle. Facial expressions and body posture are two other large pieces, and the way we fit these three puzzle pieces together determines the sub-conscious message we send with our whole bodies. Let's take a look at each of these areas to uncover how we can read and send signals with each.

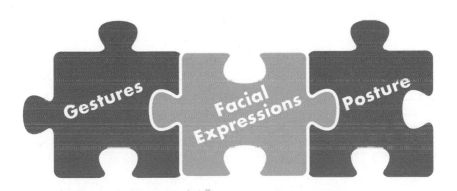

Fast Fact

If you consciously understand the visual signals you send and receive, you will be better able to connect with others on a more meaningful level.

Gestures

By gesturing with our hands and arms (and sometimes even our legs and feet) we reinforce our words and overall messages. Depending on your culture and the situation, your hands alone could be more meaningful than the words you use. Italians are famous for their gestures and body movements when they speak. I was able to experience this first hand at a birthday party for an Italian friend. I don't speak a word of Italian, but was amazed by how much I could understand just by watching the Italians there interact. In a social situation such as this, gestures were as free-flowing as the alcohol. If we had met under more professional circumstances, they might have toned down their gestures slightly. But it's hard to say — they are Italian!

 Myth Buster

All humans use body language in the same way, regardless of culture.

This is a very dangerous statement to assume! People from different cultures have different ways of using their bodies to express themselves. Be sure to acquaint yourself with a culture's norms to be sure you don't unintentionally make an insulting or embarrassing gesture. It's also important that you are familiar with their body language so that you don't misinterpret their signals either.

So what types of gestures do we make, and why? We can break gestures up into three general categories: open, closed and unintended gestures. Open and closed gestures are purposeful actions we take to reinforce our messages. Unintended gestures, on the other hand, are those we perform out of nervousness, tension or boredom.

When we use open gestures, our hands and arms are open to the people we are speaking with. By opening our gestures we are trying to show people that we have nothing to hide and that we are being honest. This openness originally stems from warriors who greeted each other by showing they were unarmed. Think of the way we wave 'hello' to people with an open hand as opposed to shaking a closed fist.

It's also important that you show both hands when you make open gestures, to signal that you are not hiding anything behind your back or in your pocket. I got away with this countless times growing up with two younger brothers. I could make fantastic promises, but always go back on them as long as my fingers were crossed behind my back. Once my brothers got a little bit older and understood the game I was playing, they would insist that I had both hands on the table before making any deals. This was especially true when we played Monopoly!

Closed gestures are generally viewed as being more negative, although it really does depend on the situation. When you first think of a closed fist, you probably think of someone wanting to start a fight. But what about a political leader who uses a closed fist during his speech to show determination, power and strength? The same is true of crossed arms. If someone is angry and crosses their arms, they are obviously tense. But there are situations where crossed arms can look relaxed, credible and confident.

Fast Fact

> When it comes to gestures, the most important thing is to be yourself. If you are at ease, your body will naturally and appropriately support your message.

Unintended gestures are those that do not add any meaning to your messages and usually appear due to nervousness, tension or sometimes plain boredom. Playing with rings, picking at or chewing nails, or playing with objects like a pen or napkin are all fidgeting gestures that you perform without thinking. Everyone has different habits and most people don't even know what theirs are. It's not until you see a photograph or video recording that you stop and think, "Why am I doing that?" When you consciously notice your bad habits, you can begin to take action to stop them.

It is interesting to note that many nervous gestures have something to do with trying to calm ourselves by touching ourselves in some way. For example, scratching your head, rubbing your neck, pinching an eyelid or eyebrow, adjusting your tie, stroking your hair or playing with your nails are all ways of self-soothing. Next time you are in a slightly uncomfortable situation, try to consciously notice if you do any of these things, and stop doing them immediately.

For more on body language, especially in relation to making presentations, check out Alison Lester's book *Present for Success*, also in the ST Training Solutions Success Skills series.

Facial expressions

One way that we are able to determine the true meaning of different gestures is by combining them with facial expressions. It's obvious that the politician with a closed fist is not trying to start a fight on stage because his facial expression is not one of anger and aggression, but one of determination. There is a huge difference, and it's one that we can all decipher immediately when we look at people. The two parts of the face that we use the most to create facial expressions are the eyes and mouth. This is why we focus so much on eye contact and friendly smiles.

If you are able to hold eye contact with your audience as a speaker, it usually shows you are comfortable with your surroundings and with your listeners. The majority of people would also find you to be honest and sincere. The speaker who can't hold (or even make) eye contact usually won't be trusted.

As a listener, it's even worse. If you can't hold eye contact, you send the message that you aren't interested in what is being said, or that the message isn't as interesting as all the other things you are busy looking at. You could also be seen as being nervous or uncomfortable. Of course there are also cultural conventions governing eye contact that should be taken into consideration. Many Asian cultures in particular limit eye contact based on gender, status or age.

The power of a smile is truly amazing. Years ago I met my husband in a crowded bar in Switzerland on a Saturday night. His pick-up line? A smile! Out of the sea of faces, I saw him looking at me with a big friendly smile and I couldn't help but smile back. The rest is history. How many people do you cross paths with every day on your way to work, on the train, in the elevator, at the café near your office or in your office itself? How many of them do you share a smile with? How many of them do you even look at? Business deals are won and lost based on how we perceive each other. Friendliness never fails — try it.

Try This

I dare you to start smiling at people. It doesn't matter who they are — your colleagues, your bus driver, the police officer on the corner, the staff at a restaurant or absolute strangers. What kind of responses do you get? Do you find that you attract more positive, friendly and open people into your life?

Danger Zone

There is a fine line between a friendly smile and a creepy, overly-flirtatious smile. Usually the difference is the length of time you hold eye contact and the strength of that eye contact. It's okay to smile and acknowledge that there are other people in this universe besides you. It isn't okay to make people feel uncomfortable by staring and smirking at them for no reason. My husband hooked me because his smile was warm, genuine and inviting, not dirty and slimy.

Posture

One of my best friends from high school, Nyrene, had a natural knack for looking good and carrying herself well. She always looked great, and we still joke today that she's perfect all the way down to her beautifully manicured finger nails. I can remember the two of us going to an event where there were going to be a lot of people we had never met before, and as image-conscious teens, we were of course a bit nervous about it. As we were walking up to the entrance, Nyrene stopped me and gave me her pep talk, "Shoulders back, chest out, chin up. We own the place!"

As funny as it sounds, I still remember Nyrene's mantra every time I need a little extra confidence when I enter a room. Managing your posture can manage your attitude, give you added confidence and make you look more open and approachable.

 Aha! Moment

Proper posture feels good! When I stand and sit up straight, I improve blood and oxygen flow, take unnecessary stress off of my shoulders and neck, and boost my physical and mental well-being.

Turning poor posture into proper posture is easier than you think. In one of my most recent workshops there was a man whose posture really worked against him. His shoulders were hunched forward and his back was rounded. His arms hung down in front of his legs instead of at his sides. This forced him to thrust his head forward so that he could look at people when they spoke to him. He spent much of his time looking at the floor. The image he was sending out was far from confident or even competent. I would never have hired him at an interview or thought that he could handle any type of responsibility.

We worked with him to get his shoulders back, straighten his spine and hold his head in a level position. It felt very strange to him, but when he got it right, the entire group gasped in amazement. He was a completely different person. When he saw himself in the mirror, he smiled a bigger smile than I had seen all day. Everyone saw a different side of him that he had been hiding under those hunched shoulders for so long.

Seven steps to perfect posture

Take a moment to assess your posture. Are you using your body to hide the true you? Here are my seven steps to changing your posture and presenting yourself as cool, confident and relaxed in any setting:

1. Pull your shoulders back in line with your spine and relax them.

2. Let your arms hang comfortably at your sides and avoid unintended gestures.

3. Open your hands and rest them next to your legs.

4. Lift your chin up so that you are looking straight ahead and not at your feet or the floor. Be careful that your chin is not so high that you look arrogant.

5. Pull your stomach in and push your hips forward so that your spine is nice and straight.

6. Place your weight evenly on both feet and avoid swaying back and forth.

7. Put on your best smile and 'own the place'!

Now you might be wondering how you could possibly look relaxed when you're thinking about all of these things, but the more you practise proper posture, the easier it will be to naturally assume this position.

Body language and human behaviour

When you really click with someone, have you ever noticed how your bodies are in sync just as much as your minds are? Watch two close friends interact as they sit in a café over coffee. When one leans forward, the other one leans forward. When one takes a sip of coffee, the other one takes a sip. When one crosses her legs, the other crosses her legs. These two people are in sync. The same is true of romantic couples as they stare deep into each others' eyes. One of them makes a move, and the other one follows suit. What's going on?

This is my favourite little quirk of human behaviour — the way we sub-consciously change our body movements to fit the people we're connecting with. There are two ways we do this: *mirroring* and *matching*.

- **Mirroring**

When we mirror someone, we are actually making the same movements as the other person as if we are looking at ourselves in a mirror. If the other person crosses her right leg over her left, you would then cross your left leg over your right in order to mirror her.

I can remember talking with a participant during a tea break at one of my workshops. We were engrossed in conversation as we each held a plate of finger food in one of our hands. Suddenly (for no real reason other than comfort) I moved my plate to my other hand. Shortly after, the participant did the same thing so that she was mirroring me.

When I noticed her make the switch, I moved my plate back again. Sure enough, she followed. I started switching my plate back and forth thinking there was no way she would keep doing this, but she did! I passed my plate back and forth five times within less than a couple minutes! She followed my movement every time.

Instead of branding her as a copycat, I realised that she must have felt really comfortable and connected speaking with me. Otherwise this wouldn't have happened. When we went back to the workshop and I got to the point where I was demonstrating these mirroring and matching techniques, I asked this lady if she knew what she was doing at break and whether she was purposely mirroring my body language. She said she had no idea, and had never heard of mirroring and matching before! She did, however, admit that she felt very comfortable speaking with me. It's not surprising that her sub-conscious reflected that comfort in her mirroring behaviour.

- **Matching**

  Matching is very similar to mirroring, but instead of creating a mirror image, you do the same thing as the other person. When you're facing them, it looks like you are doing the opposite of what they are doing. If your friend crosses his right leg, you also cross your right leg so your legs are pointing in two different directions. These matching movements can also signal a degree of connectedness with another person.

Making body language work for you

The first question I am always asked after explaining the concepts of mirroring and matching is whether or not we can 'fake it'. My answer is always the same, "Why not?" Very few people are actually aware of the funny things our sub-conscious mind knows. The few people who have some understanding of these things are usually quite successful in whatever they do. They know how to tap into other people's minds by using these small sub-conscious cues.

Myth Buster

To mirror someone, I have to copy their movements exactly.

Mirroring actions do not have to be identical. If you are forcing these movements, it can come across as rather strange to the person you are mirroring. If someone crosses her legs at the knees, you might cross your ankles. If someone is propping up his head with his hand on the side of his face, you might prop yours up with your fist under your chin. Mirroring doesn't have to be identical to be effective.

If you feel like you aren't really 'clicking' with someone, take note of their body language and make one change in your posture or gestures to mirror or match them. It could be as simple as uncrossing your arms or crossing your legs. If the other person's body is in tune with your body, their mind will soon follow as you make them feel more comfortable around you. If you normally use lots of gestures and the person you're talking to uses none at all, you could come across as over-the-top to him while he comes across as reserved to you. Try toning down your gestures, and as the other person gets more comfortable, you just might find that he comes out of his shell.

Another way I like to use body language to my advantage is to test people with it. If I want to know whether I'm really connecting with someone, such as a potential client, I'll look for signs of mirroring and matching from that person. If they are mirroring and matching me, chances are they feel comfortable and like what I'm saying. If they sit with closed posture and a straight face, I know that I need to work harder to connect with them.

Maintaining personal space

Another non-verbal cue that needs particular attention is personal space. This is especially important when you are in inter-cultural situations. I have a very negative reaction to having my personal space invaded. Living in Asia, it has been extremely hard for me to become accustomed to the close physical proximity of people. With so many people and so little land, we have no choice but to stand on top of each other in the subway or in line at the supermarket. Even so, I have to draw the line when I can literally feel someone breathing down my neck.

When I go home to visit my family in California, I notice that my comfort zone has shrunk, and I don't mind being closer than the typical arm's length away from people. Unfortunately, the Americans haven't changed, and I find that people often take steps away from me as I come too close.

Fast Fact

Encroaching on someone's personal space is the easiest way to make them feel uncomfortable and immediately break rapport.

Even in the same culture, respecting personal space is essential. Especially in cross-gender interactions in the workplace, it is best to keep your distance. If you sense any discomfort from someone, that's your cue to take a step back and give them some breathing room.

Body language goes a long way in communicating your message to your audience. If you do not pay attention to the non-verbal signals you are sending, you are not taking full advantage of your capabilities to connect with other people. By reading others' non-verbal cues you will also gain insights into how they really feel and what they really mean to say.

Body language isn't a secret code that needs to be broken — you already understand this language sub-consciously. Start using it to your advantage!

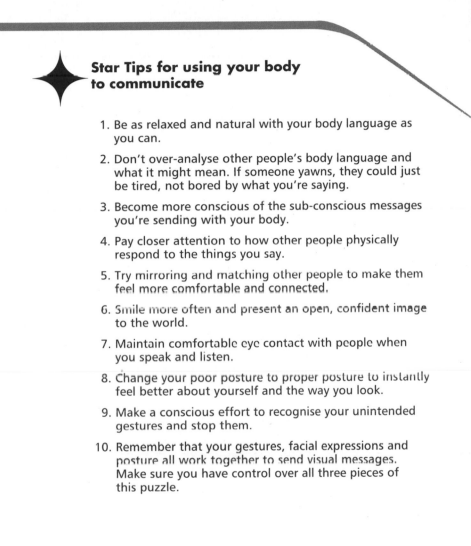

Star Tips for using your body to communicate

1. Be as relaxed and natural with your body language as you can.

2. Don't over-analyse other people's body language and what it might mean. If someone yawns, they could just be tired, not bored by what you're saying.

3. Become more conscious of the sub-conscious messages you're sending with your body.

4. Pay closer attention to how other people physically respond to the things you say.

5. Try mirroring and matching other people to make them feel more comfortable and connected.

6. Smile more often and present an open, confident image to the world.

7. Maintain comfortable eye contact with people when you speak and listen.

8. Change your poor posture to proper posture to instantly feel better about yourself and the way you look.

9. Make a conscious effort to recognise your unintended gestures and stop them.

10. Remember that your gestures, facial expressions and posture all work together to send visual messages. Make sure you have control over all three pieces of this puzzle.

MASTERING YOUR
VOICE AND TONE

*"Don't look at me in
that tone of voice!"*

David Farber

You probably put a lot of thought into what you wear and how you look when you go to work each day. You have a certain image to maintain, and your visual appearance is a huge part of that. But what about your *vocal appearance*? Does your voice support both you and your message?

What your tone of voice says about you

We usually see people before we hear them (of course, there are always exceptions). Based on how they look, we make judgements about how we think they should sound. If a person opens his mouth and his voice doesn't match the rest of his image, we get confused. I can remember the first time I heard the American boxer, Mike Tyson, speak in an interview. I was expecting a very deep, masculine and almost scary voice to come from the heavyweight champion of the world. When I heard him speak, I was shocked by his unnaturally high pitch. He sounded more like Mickey Mouse than Rocky Balboa! I found it hard to take him seriously after hearing him speak. This is a perfect (although extreme) example of how quickly your voice can affect your image.

Consider the expectations you have about people's voices. You probably expect a receptionist to have a warm, friendly tone, while the leader of a nation should sound authoritative and confident. You expect the pilot of your flight to sound experienced and capable, and radio DJs to sound smooth and cool with deep resonating voices. What if your pilot sounded like a nervous teenager flying his first plane? You probably wouldn't want to be on that flight. If the DJ had an annoying, screechy voice, you wouldn't listen to that station.

 **Aha! Moment**

My voice is an extremely important part of who I am and plays a large role in how people view me.

Myth Buster

I was born with this voice and there's nothing I can do to change it.

On the contrary! Singers, politicians and actors all invest in their voice and get coaching on how to improve it. You already adjust the way your voice sounds in certain situations without even thinking about it. You employ many different vocal attributes to send just the right message, and these attributes can be varied in order to achieve specific goals.

Vocal attributes that can hurt or help

There are many elements that come together to create the sound and power of your voice. If you are worried about the way you sound, but aren't quite sure how you can change your voice for the better, here are a few vocal attributes and the ways people normally react to them.

Pitch

Your pitch can fall anywhere on a scale from very high to very low. Lower pitches are usually perceived to be more masculine, authoritative and confident, while higher pitches are more feminine, caring and friendly. The right pitch for you will depend on your gender and profession.

If you're in the service industry, voices at the slightly higher side of the pitch scale are wonderful, because you sound happy and friendly, and make people feel comfortable. If you go too high, however, you can end up sounding young, inexperienced, nervous and insecure.

If you are in a position of authority, lower pitches will demand more respect. If you want someone to trust you, these lower pitches will also give the impression that you are knowledgeable and competent. Taken to the extreme, low voices can be viewed as extremely serious and boring. This would be the wrong pitch to use if you are any type of front-line employee who has the job of welcoming customers and clients.

Volume

If you speak too loudly, people can view you as being overly dominating and always seeking attention. On the other hand, people who speak too softly are seen as being insecure, shy and lacking confidence. Finding a happy balance for your situation is important, and having common courtesy is key. Remember that you're not the only person in the restaurant, the doctor's waiting room or the airport lounge. On the other hand, if you're at a crowded cocktail party you might just need to speak up. Depending on your situation, turn your volume up or down accordingly.

Intonation

This vocal attribute refers to the way you choose to use melody in your speech. Fluent, comfortable speech has a sing-song element to it that makes it easy and interesting to listen to. The ups and downs in tone not only add emphasis to your message (as we'll discuss in detail later), but also make you sound friendly, approachable, interesting and entertaining. People who speak in monotone are boring to listen to. Unfortunately, if you sound boring, most people will assume that you *are* boring.

Resonance

No one can forget Marilyn Monroe's seductive, breathy voice, and if you've seen the television sitcom, *The Nanny*, you will be very familiar with the screeching, nasal voice of the main character, Fran Fine. These two voices are on opposite extremes of the resonance scale. Resonance refers to the amount and location of the vibration of your voice. Marilyn used a lot of air and very little resonance to create her vocal calling card. Fran Fine, on the other hand, uses vibration in her head, and especially her nasal cavities, to create her shrill, screechy wails.

Your favourite radio DJs, whether men or women, probably have rich, resonant voices that you enjoy listening to. They sound relaxed, don't they? Relaxation is the key to great resonance. To understand why this is true, you need to know a little bit about how you create sound.

When you want to use your voice, your vocal chords begin to vibrate and they create sound. This vibration is only one small part of the quality of your voice. What really determines how your voice sounds are the cavities in which it vibrates, such as your chest, throat, mouth, and nose. The more open and relaxed these cavities are, the greater the resonance and the stronger the voice. When you are anxious, nervous or tense, your body tightens. In turn, the strength of your voice suffers because it isn't able to resonate properly. You have trouble projecting your voice and end up sounding exactly the way you feel — weak, stressed and tense.

Fast Fact

The way your voice resonates is the most important factor in how others react to your voice. Make sure that you project a voice that is in line with your image.

Pace

The speed at which you speak can have a huge effect on not only how intelligible you are, but also how your voice sounds. Very often, the faster you speak, the higher your pitch becomes. You can also come across as sounding anxious, nervous and stressed if you speak too quickly. Speeding up your speech is a natural reaction to nervous and anxious feelings. The sooner you get all our words out, the sooner you can end whichever terrible experience you are faced with: speaking in public, sitting in an interview or meeting someone on a blind date, for example.

The opposite end of the scale is no better. People who speak too slowly are usually seen as being boring, uneducated and incompetent. Their intonation ends up sounding very monotononous. Their pitch becomes low and usually doesn't resonate incredibly well. They almost sound as though they are too tired to speak properly.

Vocal attributes in action

Vocal attributes are all very important, but the way you choose to apply these attributes to your speech is how you really make magic. The key to using vocal attributes successfully is to make sure that your voice matches your message, profession and status. It should also meet the expected standard other people have set for how your voice should sound. Otherwise, people will think you sound strange — the way I felt about the boxer, Mike Tyson.

Let's take a look at a few professions, the expectations we have for them and the way that we can use vocal attributes to meet those expectations. If your job doesn't fit one of the professions on this list, don't worry. Look at the expectations we have for each, and apply the appropriate attributes to your own life.

Doctor

Our expectations: trustworthy, well-educated, competent, caring

Vocal attributes:

Pitch	Low pitches are trusted more than higher pitches
Volume	Loud enough to sound confident, but quiet enough to maintain confidentiality
Intonation	Slightly more intonation than average to sound friendly and warm
Resonance	Middle resonance that exudes confidence and warmth
Pace	Slightly quick in order to show competence about your subject, but not so quick that patients feel you don't take enough time with them

Receptionist

Our expectations: friendly, competent, good at multi-tasking

Vocal attributes:

Pitch	Higher pitch range that shows friendliness and warmth
Volume	Slightly loud to show confidence and competence, plus to help get their message across clearly
Intonation	Above average use of intonation in order to show interest in the client, friendliness, and a positive attitude
Resonance	Good resonance — a breathy voice would be unacceptable here
Pace	Slightly quick to show competence, but not so quick that you compromise clarity (especially on the phone)

Salesperson

Our expectations: knowledgeable about their product, caring of our needs, trustworthy

Vocal attributes:

Pitch	Low to gain trust
Volume	Slightly loud to show confidence and competence
Intonation	Lots of melody to show friendliness and be interesting to listen to
Resonance	Deep resonance that signals you are relaxed will help your client relax and trust you more
Pace	Slow and steady so the client doesn't feel like you are trying to trick them, and so they also feel like you are listening to their needs

Bartender

Our expectations: relaxed, easy-going, humourous, sociable, friendly

Vocal attributes:

Pitch	Lower, relaxed tones signal an easy-going attitude
Volume	Loud so people can hear you over noise and music
Intonation	Due to the high volume, your intonation will suffer, but in quieter environments, you should have a lot of intonation in order to be more entertaining
Resonance	Must have good resonance to be heard over other noise
Pace	Slow and controlled to show friendliness

It is very possible that you will find yourself in situations where you have to change from being competent and in control (perhaps when managing others) to suddenly becoming friendly and trustworthy (when speaking with clients). It's important that you understand how to take advantage of vocal attributes so that you can always exceed expectations, demand the respect you deserve and make other people feel comfortable.

 **Try This**

Consider how you might change your pitch, volume, intonation and resonance to fit the following situations. How could you use your voice to help you achieve the results you want?

- Two of your staff are having a disagreement and you need to act as a mediator.

- Your are calling a potential client for the first time and want to make a good impression.

- You are speaking to a young child who can't find his parents in a large department store.

Harmonising with others

In Chapter 5, we discussed visually mirroring and matching other people in order to form stronger bonds with them. We can, and should, do the same vocally in order to further enhance this connection. When you begin noticing how different people apply the different attributes, it will be easier for you to match their sound.

For example, if you notice that the person you are speaking with has a slower pace than you, try to slow down. If you don't, they might think you are nervous or anxious. At the same time, you might think they are lazy or ignorant. Try not to be judgemental. You most likely know more than they do about these things and can use vocal attributes effectively to build rapport and create a more successful dialogue.

You can also use vocal attributes in response to visual or verbal signals you receive from your listener. If it looks like the person you are talking to is bored by what you're saying, you might choose to speed up and end your story, or use more intonation to make what you're saying sound more exciting. You might suddenly change your volume to grab their attention, or become more or less resonant to keep them guessing your true meaning.

 Fast Fact

Our vocal attributes can be very powerful indeed. People respond more to tone than to the actual words being used. When you mix and match your vocal attributes, make sure your tone matches your message.

How your intonation can change your meaning

The way you vary your tone of voice deserves a longer discussion, because there are so many ways your tone can affect your message.

Statements and questions

First of all, it's important to recognise the way we use tone to express ourselves. Depending on the function of our sentences, our base tone naturally varies. For example:

Statement: You need to finish the report by Friday.

Your tone should be relatively even and the sentence should end on a down tone.

Question: You need to finish the report by Friday?

Your tone should rise at the end of this sentence, signalling that it is a question instead of a statement.

Danger Zone

Some people fall into the habit of raising their tone at the ends of statements. Doing so can make you sound unsure of yourself and what you're saying. Your listener thinks, "Do you know what you're talking about or are you asking me?" If you are in a position of authority, it is especially important for you to be aware of this vocal pitfall. Make sure that you are only using a rising tone at the ends of questions.

Emphasis

Another way we can vary our intonation is by changing our tone to stress different words in our sentences. Usually in order to emphasise a certain word, we raise our tone slightly. Take a look at this sentence. It is the same six words written the same six ways. The only difference is that a different word in each sentence is bold and italicised. Try reading the sentences out loud and raise your tone when you say each word in italics.

1. *She* had the best job ever.

2. She *had* the best job ever.

3. She had *the* best job ever.

4. She had the *best* job ever.

5. She had the best *job* ever.

6. She had the best job *ever*.

Did you notice how the meaning of each sentence changed when you changed your intonation? Let's look at each one in turn:

1. **She** had the best job ever.

   This sentence emphasises the person we're talking about.

2. She **had** the best job ever.

   Here we are talking about the past. Unfortunately, she doesn't have this job anymore.

3. She had **the** best job ever.

   This sentence stresses the singularity of the job and its uniqueness.

4. She had the **best** job ever.

   Now the stress is on how fantastic the job really was.

5. She had the best **job** ever.

   This sentence refers to the object of the sentence and could be clarification to someone asking the question, "She had the best **boss** ever?"

6. She had the best job **ever**.

   This final sentence emphasises how extremely good the job really was. There has never been, nor will there ever be, a better job than the one she had.

There you have it — six sentences with the same six words, but all implying something completely different. If this doesn't show the power of tone, I'm not quite sure what does!

Aha! Moment

The way I use my voice to express myself adds even more to my message than the words I use. It's not *what* I say that's important, but *how* I choose to say it!

Sarcasm

The key to powerful people skills is to make sure your visual and vocal messages match the words you are using so that you come across as being authentic. The only time you might choose to make an exception to this rule is when you are being sarcastic. Sarcasm is the result of your words and tone being obviously out of sync.

If my husband wants to be really nice, he might look at me and say, "You're so beautiful," and actually mean it. Then on a Saturday afternoon after I have been spending all day in the backyard cleaning the pool and working in the garden he might say, "You're *so beautiful*," and it's obvious he means the exact opposite.

Danger Zone

Be careful with sarcasm. It should only be used with audiences you know well, and only when you know they can handle it.

Using tone to express emotion

As we discussed in Chapter 3, many people struggle with expressing emotion. They try to hide how they really feel, but their tone usually says it all. Have you ever snapped at a loved one after having a bad day at work? I'm not sure I know anyone who hasn't. You don't mean for your words to come out that way, but the stress and tension you're feeling is suddenly mirrored in the tone of your voice.

Reading different tones is much like reading visual cues in that we have an innate capacity to understand them. Regardless of the words that are said, we know what certain emotions sound like.

 **Try This**

Open your phone book to a random page and start reading out loud. It doesn't matter if you're reading a name, address or telephone number. The point here is not to communicate with your *words*, but with your *voice*. Try to express these emotions with only your tone. Find a partner and have him guess which emotion you are communicating. Notice how you vary your vocal attributes to create the sound of each emotion.

- Anger

- Confusion

- Boredom

- Sadness

- Happiness

- Excitement

- Jealousy

- Love

It's amazing how much your voice has to say. If you've never thought about how your voice reflects you, your mood and your attitude, I hope you'll begin taking this into consideration. If you feel that your voice needs some work, don't be afraid to ask for help from a voice coach who can show you exactly how to improve your resonance, pitch, intonation, volume and pace.

Knowing how to adjust your vocal attributes to better fit the situation will help you present a more polished image and connect with others on a vocal level.

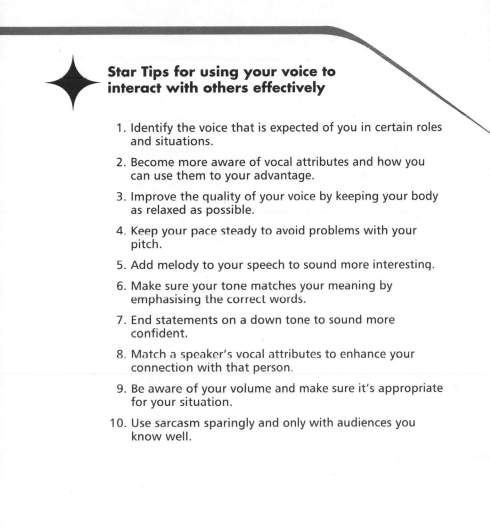

Star Tips for using your voice to interact with others effectively

1. Identify the voice that is expected of you in certain roles and situations.

2. Become more aware of vocal attributes and how you can use them to your advantage.

3. Improve the quality of your voice by keeping your body as relaxed as possible.

4. Keep your pace steady to avoid problems with your pitch.

5. Add melody to your speech to sound more interesting.

6. Make sure your tone matches your meaning by emphasising the correct words.

7. End statements on a down tone to sound more confident.

8. Match a speaker's vocal attributes to enhance your connection with that person.

9. Be aware of your volume and make sure it's appropriate for your situation.

10. Use sarcasm sparingly and only with audiences you know well.

HOW TO MAKE GREAT CONVERSATION

"A gossip is one who talks to you about others; a bore is one who talks to you about himself; and a brilliant conversationalist is one who talks to you about yourself."

Lisa Kirk

7

The non-verbal messages you send with your body language and voice are extremely important. Even so, you won't feel confident speaking in groups of people unless you know that you will always have something interesting to say. I've found that 'saying something stupid' is one of my clients' greatest fears when it comes to speaking in public — whether it's formally to a large audience, in smaller groups or one on one.

So how can you be sure to use your language correctly? In this chapter we'll discuss how to speak clearly and correctly so you can achieve more positive results in your relationships.

Your language and what it says about you

In Chapter 6 we talked about your vocal appearance and how people expect you to sound a certain way when you speak. The same is true of the language you choose to use. Your grammar and word choice say a lot more about you than you might think. Proper grammar signals a higher level of education, professionalism and, in many cases, success. Breaking grammar rules can signal a lack of attention to detail, laziness and can be a general irritant and distraction for those who make an effort to speak properly.

Your word choice sends out additional clues about your background and age. English slang words are regional and vary from city to city and country to country. Different varieties of English also have different vocabulary. For example, I call the storage space at the back of my car a 'trunk' and not a 'boot'. So when I ask my Singaporean taxi drivers to open the trunk they often exclaim, "Oh, you're American!"

I would have the same reaction if I were in America and heard people adding '*lah*' to the ends of their sentences. I would immediately know they were from Singapore, just as the ones adding '*eh?*' are most likely from Canada.

Try This

Make a list of the words or phrases you've heard or used that are geographically linked to a certain type of English. These are the words or phrases that, when you hear them spoken, immediately give away where the speaker is from, even if he doesn't have a strong accent. Which words and phrases are specific to your variety of English and could signal where you come from?

Slang words not only point to a geographic location, but can also give you an idea of someone's age. Sometimes when I talk to my youngest brother, Nic, I think we're speaking different languages. We are only four years apart, yet he uses slang words that I've never heard before. That's how quickly language changes and why you probably went through a stage growing up when your parents didn't have any idea what you were talking about.

Danger Zone

Remember that the language you use should sound natural, be your own and be appropriate for the situation. Parents trying to copy their teenagers' slang sound ridiculous because the words are not age appropriate. Using slang in the boardroom can be just as disastrous because it simply isn't appropriate for the situation.

We all use different words and phrases based on the situation and our audience. When I'm back in my hometown with the friends I grew up with, I'm sure I switch back to using the slang and phrases that we used growing up. When I'm travelling around the world and communicating with non-native English speakers, I use a completely different style of English. That's because it is important to adjust the way I speak for my listeners.

Even the language I use when writing this book has been changed to suit my readers. Although I come from the US, the immediate market for this book speaks British English. That's why you'll find British spelling, punctuation and vocabulary used throughout. Does this mean that I'm not being authentic? No. Just as I change my visual and vocal signals based on the situation, I also use my language in a way that will be most relevant to my audience. My message is still the same.

Aha! Moment

When I write or speak, I need to put a lot of thought into the language I use. I should ask myself: Is my language appropriate for my audience? Will it meet their expectations as to how someone of my age, education and status should write or speak?

Positive language gets positive results

Much of Chapter 2 focused on maintaining a positive attitude and outlook on life in order to attract more positive people to you. This also applies to your language. Many of us have negative ways of speaking and we don't even realise it. This negativity affects not only your own outlook, but also how people respond to your comments and requests. If you speak positively, you will find that you get more positive outcomes as a result.

Take for example your list of goals or resolutions for a new year. Do you write, 'Give up chocolate', or 'Eat healthy foods'? Is it 'Stop smoking', or 'Breathe freely'? Our words send a message full of imagery to our brains. If you tell yourself to give up chocolate or stop smoking, what pictures do you see? Probably your favourite chocolate treats and packs of cigarettes, right? The positive translations, on the other hand, provide images of bowls of fruit and exercising without wheezing. Positive language focuses on what we want in life instead of what we don't want.

I'm quickly learning with my daughter, Victoria, that positive reinforcement will get me a lot further than negative demands. When she throws her toy on the floor over and over again, I say, "Hold on tightly!" instead of "Stop throwing your toy!" I give her positive attention in order to get positive results. This doesn't only apply to children. If you want someone to do something for you, try phrasing what you want done in a positive statement instead of a negative demand.

For example, let's say Mary has written a report about the company's recent merger. Most of her report is fairly good, but there are three sections that are quite convoluted and unclear. There are two ways you could approach this situation:

#1   *"I've read your report, Mary. It's okay, but these three sections are really unclear. I don't think anyone will understand what you're trying to say. You're going to have to change them."*

#2   *"Mary, your report is looking good. I love the short paragraphs and clear points. Do you think you could change the three parts I've marked to match that style?"*

Which request do you think Mary will respond to more favourably? I believe she would prefer the second request that focuses on the positive points in her report and shows her that her work was appreciated. Mary would happily make the appropriate changes and be glad to have received such constructive feedback. The first request, on the other hand, would make Mary feel belittled and as though all her good work had been overshadowed by a few negatives. She would probably become more defensive of her work and wouldn't be as happy to make the changes.

Fast Fact

For every negative, there's normally a positive. You will get more positive results by focusing on positives rather than negatives whenever possible.

For more on the power of words and how they affect our relationships, do take a look at *Communication: Your Key to Success*, by Shirley Taylor and Alison Lester, also in the ST Training Solutions Success Skills series.

The art of small talk

We enjoy doing business with people we like and connect with more than people we don't. That's why the 'pot of gold' we talked about in Chapter 3 is so very important. The only way to find that pot of gold is to participate in small talk and discover the common interests we share.

Small talk is all about getting to know someone and creating a connection before getting down to the nitty gritty details. It is an important step in laying a trusting, common foundation from which to build a professional relationship.

The amount of small talk that is expected and acceptable during a business meeting differs from culture to culture. In my experience I've found there's an obvious divide between east and west. In America for example, we like to get down to business fairly quickly, and then spend more time getting to know each other after the meeting. In Asia it's the exact opposite, with great importance placed on establishing a relationship first. Once you've formed a solid relationship, you'll be able to build on it, and could have a loyal customer for life — or at least as long as you maintain the relationship.

Finding topics to talk about

One of the challenges to making small talk is knowing what to say. We've all been in a situation where we are introduced to someone new, and we go through the normal "Nice to meet you" formalities, and then... silence. What's next? Kicking off the conversation is the hardest part of small talk, especially if the person who introduced you didn't give you any idea as to what the two of you might have in common.

Here are some customary opening questions you might use when meeting new people:

"So, where are you from?"

"What do you do?"

"How do you know John and Mindy (the hosts)?"

"Where do you work?"

Hopefully one of these openings will give you something to work with. But what if you find out that your new friend, Jack, is an aeronautical engineer or has some other job description you know absolutely nothing about? Most people in this situation would just freeze and start scanning the room for the emergency exits. But instead of being embarrassed about your lack of knowledge on the subject, what if you change your attitude, and see this as an opportunity to learn something new? You could reply with, "Wow! That sounds really interesting! To be honest, I'm not sure I know exactly what that entails. What kinds of projects do you work on?" By humbling yourself, you put Jack in a position of authority and also give him permission to talk about something he's passionate about. This gets the ball rolling.

Finding a conversation-starter is always easier when you are well read and keep up with the latest news and events. You'll also have more confidence in your ability to keep the conversation going when you've kept abreast on current affairs. As an avid news reader, you might reply to Jack by saying, "Oh, aeronautical engineering! Did you attend the air show last weekend?" Or maybe you pick a different newsworthy tid bit, "So what do you think of the design of the new A380? Is it as great as people say it is?"

Have you ever noticed that interesting people usually have interesting things to say? In addition to reading more and following the news, it helps if you get out and about, try new things and meet new people. The more you've done and experienced, the greater your chances that you'll have something in common with others. If you attended the air show, you probably learnt about some recent advances in aeronautical technologies that you could talk to Jack about.

Try This

Commit yourself to trying one new thing each month. Choose things that you never would have imagined you would try. Take a ride in a hot air balloon, get certified to scuba dive, take a cake decorating class or travel somewhere new. Push yourself to step out of your comfort zone. The more you've done in life, the more you'll have to talk about.

Asking the right questions

Some people take more time than others to open up in conversations. You try to be friendly and interested in other people, but getting them to share something about themselves can be about as tough as pulling out their wisdom teeth. You ask question after question and get simple one word answers every time. You start to feel like you're interrogating the poor people and they seem to be getting more and more uncomfortable.

When this happens, stop and think about the types of questions you are asking. If you are asking closed questions — questions that can be answered with 'yes' or 'no' or a single word or phrase — the shy person will only give the information that is absolutely necessary. Open questions, on the other hand, require the person being asked to expand on what they are saying, give an opinion or provide additional information.

I caught myself in a vicious closed question-answer cycle at a conference recently:

Me: So what do you do, Catherine?

Catherine: I'm a secretary.

Me: Oh, really? Where do you work?

Catherine: The Ministry of Education.

Me: How long have you been working there?

Catherine: About eight years.

Me: Wow, that's a long time! You must like it there!

Catherine: It's alright.

Me: Do you find your job challenging?

Catherine: Sometimes.

You can see where this conversation is going — absolutely nowhere. There are two ways I could respond to this type of interaction. I could either deem Catherine as being conversationally-challenged and get away from her as quickly as possible, or I could reassess the questions I am asking and find a better way to help her open up and share more about herself.

The main problem was that all the questions I was asking were closed questions. Even though Catherine could have read into them and added additional information, she wasn't the talkative type who would jump on the chance to talk about herself. Let's see how I could have changed the course of the conversation by asking questions that would have allowed Catherine more room to express herself.

The conversation would probably start the same way:

Me: What do you do, Catherine?

Catherine: I'm a secretary.

Me.   Oh, really, where do you work?

Catherine: The Ministry of Education.

Me: How long have you been working there?

Catherine: Eight years.

This first series of questions, although closed, are necessary to get some basic background information about Catherine. Once I had this background information, I could have changed my approach.

> Me: Wow, you must enjoy it. What keeps you there year after year?

> Catherine: *I don't know. I have a lot of nice colleagues and my boss is great. We work well together.*

> Me: Your boss must be really happy with you since you've been there so long. What's the most challenging part of what you do?

> Catherine: *Probably the stress of the job. There are a lot of things to keep track of and my boss is really busy most of the time. I have to be really organised...*

This time we have lift-off! By starting with a series of closed questions and then digging deeper with open questions, Catherine has time to get comfortable before opening up to me. Positive feedback is also important to show that I am truly interested in what she is saying.

Fast Fact

Just because someone is shy or nervous does not mean he doesn't have anything interesting or important to say. A good conversationalist knows how to make people feel comfortable by asking the right questions.

Try This

What open questions could you ask as follow-ups to these closed questions?

- Do you like to play golf?
- Did you enjoy your holiday?
- Do you like your job?
- How many years have you worked as a nurse?
- Have you visited this association before?

Making people feel comfortable

In addition to asking the right questions, the language you use can also go a long way in helping to make other people feel comfortable speaking with you. Nobody wants to look dumb or be left out of a conversation.

When you are in mixed company, try to avoid using jargon or technical language. This is probably the most common conversational blunder I observe at different social and professional functions. Let's look at an example:

A group of people are standing by the punch bowl at a party, and after introductions, Mark and Josh find out that they work in the same industry. Suddenly the conversation turns to acronyms and technical terms that only they know. Kathy, Edwin and Sue look blankly at each other not knowing how to get involved in the conversation.

Another scenario is that you ask Mark an open question about the type of work he does, and he immediately dives into a world of terms you've never heard of. You suddenly feel like you can't keep up and hope he'll stop talking as soon as possible.

Myth Buster

Sharing the details of my work by using industry-specific terminology will show others how advanced and knowledgeable I am in my field.

Unfortunately, this isn't the case. By speaking in terms unfamiliar to your listeners, you alienate them and make them feel uncomfortable. The greatest, most knowledgeable teachers are the ones who can make complicated subjects simple.

Another conversational pitfall occurs when two good friends attend a large function together. Katie and Rachel have worked in the same company for four years. They just met Chris at a networking function and begin to engage in a bit of small talk. As the conversation runs dry and no one is sure what to say, Katie turns to Rachel and brings up a story about what happened in the office last week. They start gossiping about all the people they know, and Chris is stuck standing there not knowing what to do or say.

Danger Zone

It's easy to get wrapped up in private conversations with people you feel comfortable with, and forget everyone else around you. Good conversationalists stick to subjects everyone can contribute to. If telling a private story will add something to the conversation, make sure to give the appropriate background details so that everyone can follow the story and feel included.

Enough is enough

We've all met people who can talk about just about anything and, if given the chance, will do so all night long. All we want to do is politely end the conversation, change the subject or just disappear, but it seems like we'll never get the chance. You've sent all the signals — vocal cues like "Hmm...", and "Really..." in perfect uninterested monotone, you haven't made eye contact for over three minutes, and you're incredibly interested in a small scratch you discovered on the side of your watch. Still, your talker won't stop talking. Obviously he is not reading your clear signals, so you're going to have to spell it out and excuse yourself at the first opportunity.

If you ever find yourself in this situation, here are some phrases you can use:

> *"I'm sorry to cut this short, but I'm going to have to get going. I have another appointment this evening."*

> *"Well, I've sure learnt a lot this evening! It's been nice speaking with you."*

> *"Oh, look at the time! I'm going to have to get going."*

> *"I'm sure you have a lot of people to catch up with tonight. I don't want to take all your attention. Have a nice evening."*

 Aha! Moment

If people are sending visual and vocal cues that they aren't interested in what I'm saying, it might be time for me to let someone else speak!

Making great conversation doesn't have to be as scary as many people make it out to be. As was mentioned in Chapter 4, some of the best conversationalists are actually the people who talk the least! If you take a sincere interest in the people around you and ask open questions to learn more about them, you'll not only find that you click more with others, but also that they'll admire your conversational abilities. Speak clearly by avoiding jargon and regional slang, and follow general grammar conventions to come across as the professional and competent person you really are!

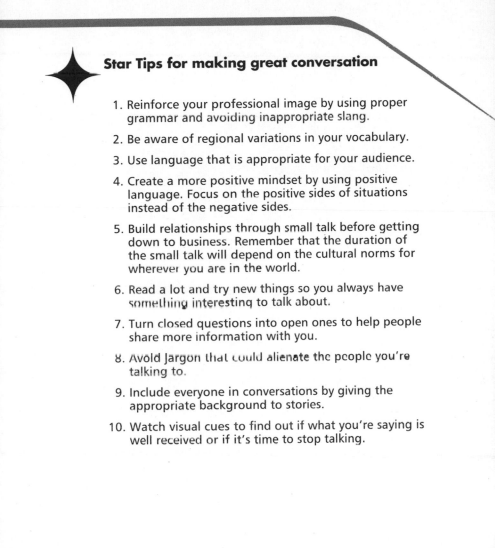

Star Tips for making great conversation

1. Reinforce your professional image by using proper grammar and avoiding inappropriate slang.

2. Be aware of regional variations in your vocabulary.

3. Use language that is appropriate for your audience.

4. Create a more positive mindset by using positive language. Focus on the positive sides of situations instead of the negative sides.

5. Build relationships through small talk before getting down to business. Remember that the duration of the small talk will depend on the cultural norms for wherever you are in the world.

6. Read a lot and try new things so you always have something interesting to talk about.

7. Turn closed questions into open ones to help people share more information with you.

8. Avoid jargon that could alienate the people you're talking to.

9. Include everyone in conversations by giving the appropriate background to stories.

10. Watch visual cues to find out if what you're saying is well received or if it's time to stop talking.

DODGING DIFFICULT SITUATIONS

"If A is success in life, then A equals X plus Y plus Z. Work is X; Y is play; and Z is keeping your mouth shut."

Albert Einstein

Even when you have mastered the content of the last three chapters — you use body language and vocal attributes perfectly, and are a better conversationalist than anyone you know — awkward moments are still bound to happen. Everyone makes mistakes. You might forget a name or can't remember where you met someone. Maybe you say the wrong thing and hurt someone's feelings unintentionally, or get caught up in a heated discussion that's going nowhere. How can you navigate through these rough seas and still hold onto good relationships, keep rapport and maintain the respect of those around you? In this chapter we'll look at some difficult situations and how to handle them successfully.

I'm sure we've met before

I was born and raised in California. Just weeks after graduating from university, I moved abroad. I make it back 'home' once a year, if I'm lucky, and stay for only two to three weeks. When I'm visiting my hometown I almost always bump into someone from my distant past and, more often than not, I am not exactly sure who the person is. I have a hard time placing the people I meet, even though I might recognise their faces.

So what should we do when people approach us and seem to know us well, and we just can't seem to remember who they are? This sticky situation is quite common, especially when you are surprised to meet someone you haven't seen for many years. Often you see the face, recognise it, and then your mind goes blank. You search and search for a name, an occupation, every club you've ever been a member of — anything that could help you to place that individual.

The biggest mistake you could make in this situation is to talk to this person without knowing who he is and hope that you'll figure it out during the course of the conversation. The further you get into a dialogue with someone, the harder it is to stop and ask, "I'm sorry. Who are you?" No matter what, be honest from the very start. There is a very small window of opportunity when we meet new people or reunite with people for the first time in many weeks, months or years, where it is acceptable to ask for the person's name and connection to you. If you miss this window, your conversation will only become more and more uncomfortable as you go on.

You might think this is acceptable only when reuniting with people after a very long absence, but this is also quite common when you run into someone outside of where you would normally see them.

I was in a situation recently where I was on holiday outside of Singapore and I saw a man who looked very familiar. We both stared at each other but neither of us said anything. I told my husband that he looked so much like the president of the Professional Speakers' Association in Singapore (of which I'm a member) but he didn't seem to react to seeing me, so I guessed it wasn't him. The next day I met him at the lift and he said, "Hi, Heather!" I looked at him and said, "I knew it was you!" It was so strange to see him outside of our monthly meetings in normal, casual clothes instead of his suit and tie. I was caught completely off guard. He was such a different person than the one I was used to seeing.

After realising that he really was the person I thought he was, I felt silly for not having said something the night before. Don't make the mistake of being afraid to approach people you might know. There is never any harm done in asking, "Are you... ?"

 Fast Fact

If you happen to mistake a person for someone else, no harm has been done. Simply apologise for bothering them and move on.

Danger Zone

Try not to take it personally if you recognise someone and approach them, only to find they don't remember you. When you approach someone you don't see on a regular basis, just say something like, "Hi, it's Maria, right?" Then introduce yourself immediately and remind her how you know each other. By doing this, you can completely avoid the awkward 'Who are you?' situation, and you give the other person the opportunity to say, "Yes, of course! I remember you!" This is a much nicer response than a blank stare and confusion as to who you are.

Forgetting someone's name

Are you one of those people who is just 'bad with names'? This is a very common excuse that I hear used all the time. In reality, you are not bad with names, but at taking the time and energy to remember names. I'm sure you have no problem remembering the names of the people who are close to you, people you really like or the names of your favourite stores and restaurants. It's easy to remember these names because you take an active interest in these people and places. If you do the same with everyone you meet, you'll find that remembering names will be much easier.

On a recent visit to a business networking meeting with a group of 15 people, there were some familiar faces, but the majority of people were new to me. I took an active interest in remembering each of their names as I met them. When the meeting began I took a moment to look around the room to be sure I had met everyone and remembered each person's name. Being able to call someone by name goes a long way in building rapport because it shows that you have taken an active interest in that individual.

Fast Fact

Your name was most likely the very first word you learnt and responded to, and has had a strong meaning for you since birth.

Try This

If you find it hard to remember names, there are many things you can do that might help. Try some of these tricks the next time you meet someone new.

- Make sure that you catch the name when it's first mentioned. Ask the person to repeat her name immediately if you miss it.

- Ask for the proper pronunciation of the name so that you hear the name said again and can practice the pronunciation yourself. Make sure you can say the name correctly.

- Use the person's name as soon as you can. For example, "Nice to meet you, Margaret."

- Associate the name with something you can remember. For a man named Don, you might think of Donald Duck. For a woman named Gina, you might think of your favourite pair of jeans. It really doesn't matter what kind of association you make, as long as it makes sense to you. (But please don't feel you have to let the other person know you are doing this!)

The good and bad of gossip

Some researchers of human behaviour have argued, "gossip is to humans what grooming is to monkeys". Gossiping is our way of connecting and bonding with each other on a deeper level. I have to say that I agree with this conclusion. Have you ever noticed how quickly you build rapport with someone when you find out that you both share a dislike of the same person, thing or organisation?

Unfortunately, this type of gossiping is probably one of the worst ways to build rapport. It is definitely the most dangerous. The world is getting smaller and smaller, and there is no way of knowing who other people know or how they feel about certain subjects.

Aha! Moment

My mother was right: "If you don't have something nice to say, don't say anything at all!"

Pulling your foot out of your mouth

So what should you do if you just said something horrible about a certain politician and his policies, just to find out that he happens to be your new best friend's brother? There is nothing you can do other than apologise profusely and sincerely, and promise not to repeat that story or opinion elsewhere. Own up to your faults and take responsibility for your mistakes. Anything less than a whole-hearted apology will only make the situation worse.

Use common sense and civility when meeting new people. It's okay to have opinions, but it's not okay to be rude, spread gossip or speak slanderously about others. Think before you speak, and make sure you know your audience very, very well before saying anything that could get you into trouble.

Danger Zone

Stay away from heated topics like religion and politics when you are in a new crowd. These are topics that people can feel very passionate about and it is easy to offend others accidentally.

My friend, Shirley, told me how she once put her foot in her mouth — big time. She, and her good friend, Sally, had just had coffee with a visitor from another country. Shirley didn't know the visitor very well, but this woman had contacted her because she was coming through Singapore and knew Shirley lived there. When coffee ended, they all said goodbye and went their separate ways, with Shirley and Sally heading for the washroom. While they were in their respective stalls with closed doors, they were having a heated discussion about the visitor, and in not such nice terms to be honest. When they walked out and approached the sinks, who did they see washing their hands? Yes, you guessed it, the woman they'd met for coffee! They had never been more embarrassed and have never forgotten this incident. Neither of them have ever had a conversation behind closed doors in the washroom since!

 Aha! Moment

People with big mouths get into trouble very easily. The smaller my mouth, the harder it will be for me to fit my foot in it!

Cooling heated discussions

Arguing in public is something to be avoided at all costs. Sometimes though, arguments are unavoidable. A friend of mine just loves arguing for the sake of arguing, and it really doesn't matter what the topic is or which side he is on, as long as it's opposing the other person. This sort of game is very petty, so please don't get wrapped up such things. No one comes out the winner when put in a situation like this. Not only will you end up feeling uncomfortable in the end, but you will also make the people around you feel uncomfortable. The longer the argument continues, the more likely you are to say something that could offend an innocent bystander, and suddenly the argument can snowball to include additional people.

If you find that you've been sucked into a debate that's becoming more heated than you'd like, swallow your pride and work your way out of it as quickly as possible. Show that you can be the bigger person by dropping the subject. If you feel this is an important issue that needs to be discussed further, try suggesting that you continue your discussion another time.

Aha! Moment

By ending an argument, I come out the winner, whether I really 'won' the argument or not!

Speaking in a (not so) foreign tongue

Sometimes you might know that you're saying something inappropriate so you switch to a different language that you think other people won't understand. This is a very dangerous practice! No matter how small your country or dialect group, never assume that you speak a secret code that no one else knows.

I'm not proud to say that my husband and I have fallen into this trap a couple times. Peter comes from Denmark, and only about five million people speak the Danish language worldwide. I happen to be one of them since I lived in Denmark for a few years. Danish is closely linked to Swedish and Norwegian, and speakers of one language can usually understand speakers of the other languages.

In Singapore we usually assume that we're pretty safe speaking Danish. There's only about 1,500 Danes living here and the Swedish and Norwegian populations aren't much larger. Still, it seems like every time we decide to talk about the people next to us in a restaurant or walking by in a store, they just happen to come from one of the Scandinavian countries!

Myth Buster

If I speak a rare language I can get away with being less than polite because no one can understand me!

Don't learn this lesson the hard way. Be considerate no matter what, even if you don't think anyone around you would ever understand what you're saying.

Sometimes I can be on the receiving end of this rudeness as well. When people meet me they never guess that I have a university degree in German and speak Danish fluently. In fact, even when I tell them, they usually don't believe me! I generally don't broadcast this knowledge without reason, so it's good that the two German mothers at my daughter Victoria's swimming lessons haven't said anything negative about me or, much worse, about Victoria! I have, however, heard some interesting stories that they might not have shared so openly had they known I could understand them.

It is always easier to avoid an awkward situation than have to overcome one. By being a generally nice and polite person, you will never find yourself in many of the difficult situations outlined in this chapter. Sometimes, however, difficult situations can't be avoided, such as when you forget a person's name. Remember that honesty is always the best policy and people are usually happy to help you out of a sticky situation.

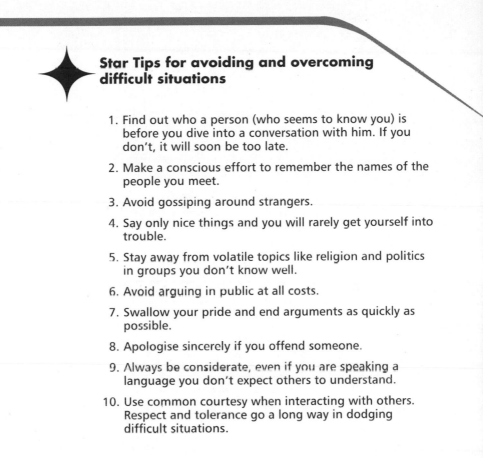

Star Tips for avoiding and overcoming difficult situations

1. Find out who a person (who seems to know you) is before you dive into a conversation with him. If you don't, it will soon be too late.

2. Make a conscious effort to remember the names of the people you meet.

3. Avoid gossiping around strangers.

4. Say only nice things and you will rarely get yourself into trouble.

5. Stay away from volatile topics like religion and politics in groups you don't know well.

6. Avoid arguing in public at all costs.

7. Swallow your pride and end arguments as quickly as possible.

8. Apologise sincerely if you offend someone.

9. Always be considerate, even if you are speaking a language you don't expect others to understand.

10. Use common courtesy when interacting with others. Respect and tolerance go a long way in dodging difficult situations.

MAINTAINING STRONG RELATIONSHIPS

*"Make new friends,
but keep the old;
Those are silver,
these are gold."*

Joseph Parry

9

Meeting, greeting and clicking with people is essential to building new relationships. But what about the relationships you already have? What actions can you take to maintain your relationships, overcome setbacks and strengthen the ties that bind you?

Whether professional or personal, sustaining strong, long-lasting relationships can be challenging. And it's an even greater challenge to maintain the relationships that mean the most to us. Staggering divorce rates all over the world can attest to that, and I'm sure that most of us have been through the heartbreaking process of falling out with a close friend. The repercussions of ending a professional relationship can also be severe, and can affect your career, reputation and maybe even your wallet.

From the moment you meet someone new, you are beginning to lay the foundation for your shared relationship. I have always felt that strong

relationships are based on three prerequisites: trust, open communication and respect. If you focus on these building blocks, you are more likely to build strong, stable, secure relationships in the long term.

Building trust from the ground up

Save yourself a lot of trouble in your relationships, and always tell the truth. When you meet someone new and have no idea what or who he knows, even the smallest white lie or exaggeration can come back to haunt you. It really isn't hard to check someone's facts. An Internet search will reveal more about you than you would probably like, and if people find out through other means that you are not all you make yourself out to be, they will question your motives and ethics. Breaking trust in this way, before you even get the ball rolling, will give you little to no chance of developing a successful relationship.

 Myth Buster

If you don't tell me it's a secret, I should be able to tell whomever I please!

This could not be farther from the truth. Based on the type of relationship you have with someone, you should instinctively know what information should be kept private. It could be good news (a pregnancy), bad news (a layoff), or an embarrassing situation (a cocktail party where someone had one too many martinis). Whatever the situation, knowing when to keep your mouth shut will earn you the trust and respect of your colleagues and friends. If you're ever in doubt, ask before you share!

Danger Zone

In addition to what you say about yourself, be careful what you say about other people. If you are constantly telling me private details about other people's lives, it will be hard to trust you with information about mine. Gossips are not hard to find. Every company, group of friends or any other type of association has one member who can't be trusted with a secret — and everyone knows it. Don't be that person!

Giving your best through open communication

When you have trust in a relationship it is much easier to communicate openly with each other. No mature adult is interested in playing games. If you have something to say, just say it. By being open and honest and expecting the same behaviour from others, you give your relationships room to grow in different dimensions. At the same time, the importance of empathy — connecting with people on an emotional level — should not be forgotten.

Many people have difficulty talking about their emotions, but emotions can be seen and heard through both visual and vocal cues, as you read in Chapters 5 and 6. And as was mentioned in Chapter 3, you will be a much more successful communicator if you empathise with others by paying special attention to these signals before, during and after you speak.

Danger Zone

Being open and honest does not mean that you should be blunt or abrupt. An important part of all communication is using empathy and being sensitive to other people's feelings. We can be open and at the same time be tactful, thoughtful and caring.

Keeping the communication lines connected

A long time ago, in a world very different than today's, people put a lot of time, effort and care into maintaining contact with those they loved. They chose the proper stationery, just the right pen, and spent quite a lot of time writing pages of heart-felt prose. Then they would seal the envelope and send their letter by boat over the oceans so the object of their affection could receive it, sometimes weeks, if not months, later.

The last real, hand-written letter I received (in an envelope and with a stamp on it) was written by my 90 year-old grandmother about a year before she passed away. Despite her failing eyesight, she managed to fill four pages with musings about her daily life plus friendly queries about mine. When I told friends about my letter, they were in awe. Firstly, because they couldn't believe that a 90 year-old could still accomplish such a feat. And secondly because, "Who actually writes letters anymore?"

Since one of the building blocks of relationships is open communication, it is important to keep our communication lines open and connected by staying in touch with the people we care about. In today's e-world, our messages are received almost immediately. We have also come to expect a reply within 24 hours, so we have few real excuses for losing touch with our contacts.

Even though our modes of communication have changed, our expectations from others haven't. In fact, in many cases we have higher expectations since it's so easy to get in touch in a multitude of different ways. The time and effort we need to expend is also minimal. Every relationship is different, and the needs of each person change over time and depending on the situation.

It is important in every relationship that you meet each other's expectations. If one person in the relationship writes once a week and expects a reply immediately, and the other only writes back once every second month, someone will most likely get hurt. I have very good friends who I talk to as little as twice a year, and when we finally see each other, we pick up exactly where we left off. Other friendships and professional relationships require more attention. Everyone is busy, but if a relationship is meaningful enough, you will make the time to do your part in keeping it alive and meeting the other person's need for attention and support.

Try This

Make a list of your most meaningful relationships. When is the last time you've been in contact with these people? Block out some time — maybe an afternoon, or maybe just one hour — to contact each person by phone, letter, e-mail or social networking site. Don't take your relationships for granted. Remind people how much you care.

Myth Buster

I should only get in touch with friends when my life is going well, and when I have positive things to say.

On the contrary! No one wants to be a burden on their friends, but if you only get in touch to brag about your accomplishments, what are you actually giving to the relationship? True friends are there for you through good and bad times, and are willing to share more than just the superficial triumphs. American singer, Dinah Shore put it best: "Trouble is part of your life, and if you don't share it, you don't give the person who loves you enough chance to love you enough."

Showing respect in your relationships

By being honest and open in your dealings with people, you are respecting their intelligence as well as your relationships. We can, and should, respect our friendships on other levels too, by taking a contact's feelings, opinions, culture and basic essence seriously. Let's take a look at each of these elements in turn.

Feelings

It is always important to respect other people's feelings with our words and actions. As you get to know people on a more personal level, you learn how they feel about and react to different things. I have some friends who are very sensitive, and I know that I need to word my opinions carefully so as not to upset them. As a leader, it's a good idea to get to know your staff individually to find out how best to approach them with feedback and suggestions. By respecting the people around you and their feelings, you not only build stronger relationships, but you will also get better results. You will make people want to do things for you because they respect you in return.

Opinions

There is nothing worse than when you ask a friend for his opinion and then completely disregard it, judge it or trivialise it. People who voice personal opinions are making themselves vulnerable. You do not necessarily have to agree with what is being said, but do be respectful in your responses.

Appropriate responses may be:

"That's an interesting point."

"I hadn't looked at it that way."

"I'm glad you mentioned that."

If you disagree with the person's ideas, you might follow up this positive response with something that points to the issue and not the person:

> *"I'm afraid I disagree with you on that point."*

> *"I'm not sure I can agree with you there."*

> *"Even though you bring up an interesting point, I'm not sure I agree with it completely."*

Inappropriate responses are any that demean the person or their thought processes:

> *"That's just stupid."*

> *"Are you serious?"*

> *"Your ideas never work."*

> *"I don't know where you get these crazy ideas!"*

 Aha! Moment

When I have a disagreement, it is not the person I disagree with but the issue at hand. By keeping the two separate, I can focus on the message without disrespecting the messenger.

Culture

Everyone deserves to be shown equal respect regardless of race, religion, language and country of origin. Just because someone does something or believes in something different than you, does not mean that she deserves less respect. By learning more about the different cultures of our world, you will grow as a person and learn new ways to view the world around you.

Basic essence

Have respect for those around you. You don't have to know someone well, or at all, to show them respect. If for no other reason, show respect for people because they are sharing the same space with you. A simple smile, holding a door or elevator, moving out of the way when walking down the street — these are all simple ways of acknowledging the existence of those around you. Everyone deserves to be shown common courtesy regardless of your relationship.

Keeping things in balance

Honesty, communication and respect work both ways in our relationships. There is a certain amount of balance that is always expected. If one person is honest and the other isn't, trust is broken. If one person is open with his communication and is always reaching out to stay in touch, and the other doesn't respond, it's hard to keep the relationship alive. And if there isn't mutual respect, there really isn't much of a relationship at all.

I can remember in my first romantic relationships as a teenager, keeping track of who called whom. I would think, "I called him yesterday, so he can call me today!" As immature as it sounds, don't we think the same things as adults? For example: "Well, we invited them over last weekend, so it's their turn to have us over for dinner next time." There is an unspoken rule that we should all give and take equally in our relationships, and if there is a significant imbalance, the relationship will suffer.

Handling relationship challenges

The primary challenge to maintaining a strong relationship is knowing how to meet the interpersonal needs of the other person, while at the same time having your own needs met. It's quite a paradox when you consider that we need others for survival (both literally and figuratively) yet the bottom line is, as humans, we are mainly interested in ourselves. This is when the 'me mentality' begins to kick in. Power and ego ruin more relationships than anything else, yet we are naturally hard-wired to be most concerned with our own advancement, success and survival.

From the moment we meet someone we try to figure out where we rank in relation to him financially, socially and professionally. Is he a threat? Could he exert any power over me? There is nothing wrong with this process, and, in fact, it is necessary for us to consider these factors in order to appropriately adjust our actions and behaviours. In this way, we can better achieve a desirable outcome. Our relationships, however, will suffer when the 'me mentality' stands in the way of fulfilling either party's interpersonal needs.

Power

Let's imagine you are currently unemployed and decide to go to a job fair. At the lunch buffet, you strike up a conversation with Michael, who is waiting next to you in line. As the conversation advances, you find out Michael is the recruiter for a company you are very interested in working for. In this specific situation, Michael has more power than you do because he could get you a job! You immediately change your behaviour to suit the situation, and as your relationship advances with this person, you will always remember in the back of your mind that Michael has some degree of power over you.

Power can be a relationship breaker when the person holding the power abuses it. Knowing that he is in a powerful position, Michael could be arrogant or disrespectful towards the people he has power over. This is how people with poor interpersonal skills might behave. If Michael does not have respect for job-seekers, he will have trouble finding the best candidate during interviews, because interviewees will have trouble opening up to him or connecting with him.

Fast Fact

People only have power because others recognise it and give it to them. Power can be taken away just as quickly as it is given, and is often taken away when it is abused.

The importance of power in our relationships can be seen every day in just about every office in the world. There are so many power struggles in the manager-employee relationship, as well as unsuccessful attempts to fulfil each other's interpersonal needs.

As an external consultant going into companies, I see, from an objective perspective, how these struggles affect the working environment and camaraderie among staff. The most successful leaders are those who can accept their power and then remove it from their interactions.

One of my clients said about his boss, "I really like working on Erik's team because he values our input. He does everything he can to help me succeed and learn more." Erik has done everything right. Instead of ruling from on high, he has taken his staff's interpersonal needs into consideration. He makes them feel included in the team and allows them to contribute. At the same time, he controls the situation enough that he can give his staff the guidance and direction they expect and need from their leader. By doing so respectfully, his staff also appreciate this guidance and view it as support instead of demands or instructions.

Another client told me that her boss would ask her opinion and then shoot down her ideas every time. Eventually she wasn't interested in contributing anymore. In this case, my client's need to feel included was not being met. She did not feel as though she was able to contribute to meeting the goals of the company. As a result, she was not very motivated. In the end, she quit her job and accepted an offer with a competitor who recognised her potential.

Aha! Moment

The saying is true: 'People don't quit bad jobs — they quit bad managers.' If I lead others without paying attention to their interpersonal needs, I will lose my greatest assets — my staff and their dedication.

Fast Fact

The whole point of developing your people skills is so you can better understand how to approach situations and adjust your behaviour to achieve a desirable outcome. If you are not aware of other people's needs, it will be hard for you to fulfil your responsibilities in your relationships.

Calling it quits

Sometimes, no matter what you do, relationships just aren't meant to be. In a professional situation, the person with less power will either end up being fired (for good or bad reason) or she will regain her power by quitting and finding a better opportunity elsewhere. Friendships will usually dissolve naturally, while marriages require a formal process. No matter how or why you are ending a relationship, it's always wise to do so amicably if possible. It will make the situation more comfortable for you and everyone around you.

When relationships break down, there may be pressure on others to choose sides. This often happens in a divorce or when two close friends in common social circles go their separate ways. It can also happen in a professional setting where people are no longer expected to support a certain individual's ideas or advancement. It's never a good idea to force people to take sides. In doing so, you spread your negativity and involve more people than necessary in your personal conflict. The situation becomes uncomfortable for everyone.

 Aha! Moment

Just because I can't get along with someone doesn't mean other people can't. Although this might be hard for me to understand, I have to respect other people's rights to associate with whomever they choose.

Myth Buster

When I end a relationship, it's best not to have any contact with that person ever again.

Although this sometimes seems like the best answer, it isn't always the most beneficial if other parties are involved. If you work with that person, you'll need to find a way to get along in your office. If you have children with the person, you'll have to be able to communicate about issues regarding them. Sometimes you can continue a relationship by creating more distance between you, without actually cutting off all contact.

When I lived in Denmark, I was amazed when I heard about a divorced couple who would spend Christmas together every year. At first I thought it must only be this one crazy couple, but when I dug deeper, I found that many split families came back together to celebrate holidays, graduations, confirmations and any other events that involved their children. And if one or both partners were in new relationships, their new partners would also be invited. This was much different than what I am accustomed to in the United States where divorced couples will rarely look at each other, let alone speak or celebrate special occasions together!

I'll never forget the answer I received when I asked my friend how she could actually stand being in the same room with her ex and his new girlfriend. She just gave me a strange look and said that they were still the parents of their children, and the kids should be able to enjoy them both. She said that they respected their differences and supported each other in finding happiness. Wow! How refreshing.

What if we could be this open, honest and accepting in all our relationships? What if we could bottle up all the hurt, pain and deceit that leads up to ending a relationship and throw it out to sea, never to be felt again? How much of our lives are wasted holding onto the bitterness, anger and betrayal of days gone by?

Try This

When you recognise that a relationship needs to end, try to end it cordially. Hold no grudges. You'll live a fuller and healthier life and be better able to maintain the other more meaningful relationships you're involved in.

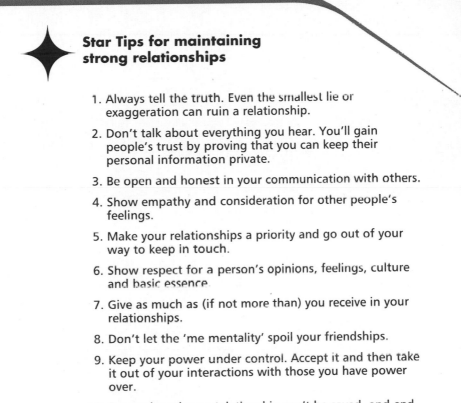

Star Tips for maintaining strong relationships

1. Always tell the truth. Even the smallest lie or exaggeration can ruin a relationship.

2. Don't talk about everything you hear. You'll gain people's trust by proving that you can keep their personal information private.

3. Be open and honest in your communication with others.

4. Show empathy and consideration for other people's feelings.

5. Make your relationships a priority and go out of your way to keep in touch.

6. Show respect for a person's opinions, feelings, culture and basic essence.

7. Give as much as (if not more than) you receive in your relationships.

8. Don't let the 'me mentality' spoil your friendships.

9. Keep your power under control. Accept it and then take it out of your interactions with those you have power over.

10. Recognise when a relationship can't be saved, and end it cordially.

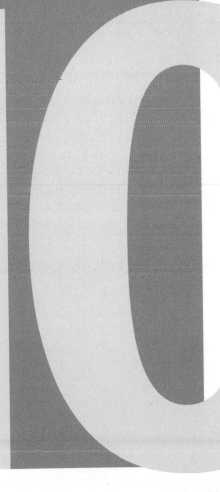

RELATIONSHIPS IN THE ELECTRONIC AGE

"The Internet is becoming the town square for the global village of tomorrow."

Bill Gates

Electronic communication channels have hugely changed the way we interact with the people in our lives. The Internet and its many new social media applications have enabled us to create limitless networks of friends, colleagues, acquaintances and even strangers. Along with these new types of relationships has come a new set of rules governing how we are expected to act and interact with others online.

Not so surprisingly, many of the considerations you take when interacting in your offline relationships are mirrored online. People still have the same interpersonal needs whether you're face to face or communicating through a computer.

Online communication and relationship building

Before we can take a closer look at the rules governing our online interactions, it's important that we understand the many different communication channels that are available, the applications that support them and what their basic uses are. This list is far from comprehensive and new applications are being developed every day that change the way we interact online. Even so, this list serves as an introduction to some of the terminology and applications we'll discuss throughout this chapter.

E-mail

This is the most common electronic tool for maintaining our personal and professional relationships. Although a comparatively simple technology, e-mail is so important to us that we've created applications for other mobile devices so we never have to go without access to our e-mail accounts. We are fully accessible to everyone (including our bosses) 24 hours a day!

Using e-mail to maintain our relationships could be a book in itself, and actually, it is. If you are interested in learning guidelines to help you use e-mail appropriately in your relationships, be sure to pick up a copy of Shirley Taylor's book *E-mail Etiquette*, also in the Success Skills series.

Forums

You can find online forums for just about any topic imaginable. Forums are an online discussion board for people sharing similar interests. You can leave comments, ask and answer questions or start a new discussion on a topic you're interested in.

Instant messenger

Unlike forums and e-mail where there is a waiting period for you to receive responses, messenger programs operate in real time. You can send short messages to any of your friends who are also online and they can respond immediately. There are many different messenger programs including Windows Live Messenger, AOL Instant Messenger, Google Talk and Yahoo! Messenger.

Computer calling

Many of the instant messenger programs now have the added function of free voice and video calling from computer to computer. Other applications like Skype have this as their base service with instant messaging as an added bonus. For someone like me who lives far away from home, Skype is a highly valued tool for keeping in touch with friends and family.

Virtual worlds

Virtual worlds are in some cases just as complex as our real world. Individuals interact with the help of 'avatars' (digital characters that look like animated versions of real people), and they can speak through text and sometimes even voice. The most popular virtual world today is Second Life. In this world, you can shop at many of the same stores you'll find at the mall down the street. You can visit your favourite politician's campaign office. You can even attend courses or company meetings online (if your company embraces this technology).

Online content sharing

There are many sites online that allow you to share your favourite music, videos, articles or other content with your selected group of friends. Sites like YouTube (for video), Flickr (for photos) and Slideshare (for presentations) let you post your own content, comment on others' content and rate your favourites. These types of sites can be very powerful for business because they offer the opportunity to take advantage of viral (word-of-mouth) marketing. It's common sense that when someone likes something, they're going to tell all their friends about it.

Blogs

Blogs have also changed the face of online communication. Blogs are basically smaller websites (although it's now possible to make them as fully-functional as a normal website) where people can post short articles and musings on anything they are interested in writing about. Sites like Blogger, Wordpress and Typepad offer interfaces for creating free blogs. Anyone can have a blog, from the stay-at-home mom to the corporate CEO. They are interactive in the sense that the content is available to anyone online and readers can leave comments which the author can then respond to. If you really like the content of a particular blog, you can sign up to receive updates to that blog directly.

Micro-blogs

Micro-blogging is a relatively new twist on the common blog. Instead of writing short articles, authors write one line of text (maximum 140 characters) which is then sent to anyone who is 'following' their updates. Twitter is the most popular micro-blogging application, and we have yet to see exactly what its future uses will be. People are already using Twitter in creative ways. Twitter groups have been formed that resemble traditional forums, just with shorter posts. Programs are available that allow you to post an update through your mobile phone as well. Many businesses are incorporating micro-blogging into their marketing mix to send short comments about their products and services to the masses. Micro-blogging is proving to be the next generation of relationship building on the Internet.

Social networking

The advent of social networking sites such as Facebook, LinkedIn, MySpace, Orkut, Hi5, Friendster, Bebo, Ning and many others, has created an entirely new universe of social interaction, and has enabled us to connect with people around the world with unprecedented ease. If you are not familiar with the term 'social networking' or are not personally involved in this revolution, there are a number of ways you can jump right in, and I'd recommend doing so sooner rather than later.

At the time of printing, the three big social networking sites are Facebook, MySpace and LinkedIn. LinkedIn is primarily a site for business professionals to network, interact and send each other business leads. Facebook is a more social application where you can post pictures and videos. MySpace is also a more social site that has come to be known as a place for music-lovers to discuss and publicise their favourite bands.

On social networking sites, you are able to connect with your offline friends and build an enormous network of people you know (and don't know) literally overnight. These sites are revolutionising the way we build virtual relationships and also how we bridge our offline relationships to the online world in order to better maintain them. This process of connecting and how we go about it is what I would like to focus on most in this chapter.

Fast Fact

Interactive online applications that allow you to build social networks and share content are collectively known as 'social media'.

Finding new friends online

When you begin building an online network, the people that you connect with can be broken down into five groups:

1. People you know and converse with on a regular basis

These are your close friends, family members and possibly some of your colleagues. You don't go more than a few days without sending them an e-mail or text message, giving them a call or seeing them in person.

2. Acquaintances and business colleagues

These are people you know, but not very well. You are selective with the information you share about yourself with these people, and wouldn't want them knowing every detail of your personal life, or seeing that picture of you singing drunken karaoke at a private birthday party.

3. People you know from long ago

Social networking sites give us the opportunity to reconnect with old classmates, long lost loves, estranged family members and old colleagues we've lost touch with. You probably don't have e-mail addresses for these people or even know how you could go about finding these old friends through any other means.

4. Strangers with common interests

Sometimes you end up connecting and creating relationships with people who share your interest in music, the arts, business, collectables, or whatever you like to spend your time doing. These relationships can be very fulfilling, and there are many people out there that are happy to exchange knowledge and information in these types of relationships.

5. Complete strangers

I recently received a friend request on Facebook from a retired professional ice skater. I have no idea how she even found me, let alone why she'd want to connect with me. I can't find anything in her profile that gives me any clue as to what we might have in common or why she's contacted me. Maybe she's confused me with someone else, or perhaps someone mentioned my name to her. It's hard to say. Sometimes people are just looking for friends anywhere they can find them.

When you register with a social networking site and start building your list of friends, you usually start with group number one: your close friends and family. Most of these sites have a tool where you can check your address book for people you know who are already using the service. You can send a personal invitation to those who aren't already online asking them to join and connect with you.

Whenever you send a request to connect, you will have the option of writing a short personal message. With your closest friends and family it isn't absolutely necessary to write a personal note, although it is a nice touch. If you're as close as you think, they should recognise your picture and know your name.

Writing a message becomes more important as you send requests to connect with relationship groups three to five. Don't assume that someone you haven't seen since elementary school will recognise your current photo or remember you at all, for that matter! It is important that you write your full name (with maiden name, if appropriate) and how you know the person (or heard of the person) in your invitation to connect.

Personally, I never accept requests to connect from people I've never heard of or seen before unless they give me some idea as to who they are and how they know me. More than any other reason, I just find it creepy! If, on the other hand, you write to me and say that you came across my website and enjoyed reading some of my articles, or, even better, that you just love this book and can't wait to learn more (flattery always works), then I'll usually connect with you. I might not give you access to view my personal photos or other personal details, but I'm happy to meet new people and expand my professional network.

 Try This

If you are not yet using a social networking site, pick one and create a free profile. Use the site's address book function to find out who from your offline network is already online and connect with them. Then, let the fun begin! While you're there, look me up, and send me an invitation to connect (including your personalised message, of course).

The status update and what it says about you

Almost all social networking sites have a 'status update' feature; in fact, micro-blogging applications like Twitter are entirely based on this concept. The point of a status update is to let your network know, in about a sentence or less, what you are currently doing personally and professionally. From what you're eating for breakfast, to what project you're currently working on in the office, these status updates are closely followed by your network and give you the chance to interact with people in a short, easy and fun way.

 Myth Buster

No one really cares about what I'm doing, feeling or working on right now.

You would be surprised how many people are interested! People are naturally nosey, and the status update gives the people in your network a glimpse into your everyday life — what you like and dislike, what you enjoy doing and how you spend your time. Through status updates you tend to uncover common interests that you have with other people that you never knew about before. This helps you build rapport and a stronger bond with others.

What to include in status updates

Remember that status updates are public domain and, depending on the service you're using, could show up in search results. Just about anyone will be able to view this information, so keep it G-rated. You also don't want to write anything you wouldn't want broadcast to thousands of people you do and don't know.

Business-savvy people take advantage of status updates to promote their products and services, using them as a sort of very short press release. For example:

"Working on my new book" (yes, I've been using this one a lot lately)

"Updating my blog" (followed by a live link to the new blog posting)

"Finishing my proposal for Company XYZ"

"Working with a new client on presentation skills training"

 Danger Zone

Be careful not to fill your status updates with marketing messages all the time. Blatant and constant self-promotion is frowned upon and is a great way to lose friends who aren't interested in your ego.

Other uses for status updates

You can also use your status updates to ask for advice, guidance or leads. I have seen many friends announce through their status updates that they were looking for a job. Several managed to land new jobs by tapping the people in their network who, in turn, tapped their networks. This is what social networking is all about.

One final way to use the status update is to share your knowledge or new resources you've discovered with your network. From useful links to funny videos and interesting business articles, offering something to your network keeps people coming back for more. Eventually you'll be seen as a resource for great content, and people will watch for your updates. When you share interesting things, your friends are also more willing to share their knowledge and lend you a hand when you need it most.

The speed of social status change

In the world of social media, celebrities are born overnight. It's amazing how quickly you can build a base of followers and become a self-proclaimed guru in your own right. I follow a 14 year-old techie on Twitter who dishes out amazing technology tips every day. He has a huge following in Singapore and around the world. Most likely, no one would have ever heard of him if it weren't for the platform that social media applications present.

At the same time, don't trust everything and everyone online. We generally believe that things we read and see in print, whether online or off, hold some degree of credibility. This isn't always true in the world of social media where just about anyone can create a blog, write articles (or have them written for a nominal fee by ghost writers) and build a large social network of followers. Luckily, people with inaccurate and useless content usually get discovered as quickly as they made a name for themselves, and the community drops them in the end. That's how powerful social media applications are.

Of course, on the flip side, if you do have something worthwhile to share, are interested in creating a larger business network, would like to find work in a foreign country, or just have a great sense of humour and want to share it, you can go from being an unemployed slacker to an online socialite in a matter of weeks, if not days.

Managing online relationships

Depending on your social media goals, you may decide only to connect with friends and family in order to update them with your personal happenings. If you are more business-focused, you might try to build a network of other professionals in your industry. Entrepreneurs will want to find potential clients and customers who will spread the word about their business, products and services.

No matter your goals, you still need to follow a set of unspoken rules when interacting with your online contacts. Here's my top 10:

1. Respond to direct messages in a timely fashion (think of them as another form of e-mail).

2. Check your social networking accounts regularly, and keep your personal information updated.

3. Give more than you take. Freely offer your help, services and resources.

4. Limit your marketing and self-promotion.

5. Be authentic. There's no reason to put on a show. People will uncover your true colours sooner than you think.

6. Be respectful in your language, viewpoints and arguments. People are happy to enter into debates, but keep things civil.

7. Just as in offline relationships, avoid gossiping and bad-mouthing others.

8. Don't participate in discussions or comment on other people's statements, photos or videos when you are upset or emotionally charged. If you think it's easy to send a heated e-mail, it's even easier to post a short comment that you could regret.

9. Be careful with humour and tone. When everything is in print and there are no visual or vocal cues, it's easy for people to misunderstand your meaning.

10. Treat people with the same respect and empathy as you would if you were sitting with them face to face. Just because the relationship is online doesn't mean it's not real.

The problem with online social networks is that so much of what goes on in them is public. If you have a fall-out with a friend or colleague on a social network, it's not just between the two of you. Suddenly everyone in both your networks can comment on the situation and rumours can spread quickly. This is why these unspoken rules are so important. In online social networks, you must always be on your best behaviour.

Maintaining online privacy and safety

The main concern I hear from people who are not involved with social networking sites is that they are afraid of strangers getting hold of their personal details, seeing their pictures and learning too much about them. Who knows what they could do with all that information! This is a very valid argument, and that's why it is so important to make your online safety and privacy a priority.

When you join a social networking site, take some time to familiarise yourself with that site's privacy controls. You usually have a lot of control over who sees what. By setting your privacy controls appropriately, you can have the same types of relationships online as you do offline. You can ensure that the photos from your wild night out on the town are only seen by your friends — and not your boss. You can also be sure that only close friends and family can view the pictures of your young children. No strangers allowed.

Remember to limit the amount of personal information you provide as well. I am shocked when I see friends list their home addresses and telephone numbers. If someone really needs your address, they can always send you a private message and ask for it. There's no reason to put that information on your profile, even if you've restricted access to it.

In addition to putting privacy controls on your own content, check what kind of control you have over other people's content that includes you. For example, if people are posting pictures of you or commenting on you in their posts, can you control who gets a public update about those actions? Often you can.

Aha! Moment

I'm not the only one posting content about me! I should pay attention to what my friends, family and other contacts are posting for the world to see. I can go into my site's privacy settings to control who sees what.

It may take some time to learn the ins and outs of your social networking platform, but you'll be glad you made the effort. The bottom line is that you should never share more about yourself than you feel comfortable with.

Moving online relationships offline

If you really get involved in social networking, you will most likely be faced with invitations from your online friends to meet offline. I have enjoyed meeting some of my online acquaintances offline, but I always exercise caution and use common sense. No matter how well you think you know a person online, unless you are a hacker, you can never be one hundred per cent certain that the person you've been communicating with is the same person you will meet in real life.

Always meet online connections in a safe, public place where you know many people will be around, and don't move too quickly in your relationship. It's easy to have a false sense of security online and think you know someone well. Treat offline meetings as what they are: the first time you're meeting a new person.

Social media applications offer many exciting opportunities to make new friends and maintain your offline relationships in new, creative ways. Choose the appropriate applications for you and your network that will meet your personal or business needs. Your powerful people skills will be just as appreciated in this online domain as they are offline.

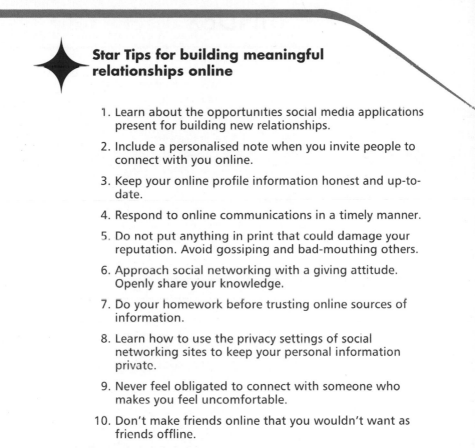

Star Tips for building meaningful relationships online

1. Learn about the opportunities social media applications present for building new relationships.

2. Include a personalised note when you invite people to connect with you online.

3. Keep your online profile information honest and up-to-date.

4. Respond to online communications in a timely manner.

5. Do not put anything in print that could damage your reputation. Avoid gossiping and bad-mouthing others.

6. Approach social networking with a giving attitude. Openly share your knowledge.

7. Do your homework before trusting online sources of information.

8. Learn how to use the privacy settings of social networking sites to keep your personal information private.

9. Never feel obligated to connect with someone who makes you feel uncomfortable.

10. Don't make friends online that you wouldn't want as friends offline.

INDEX

ABOUT THE AUTHOR

Heather Hansen has helped hundreds of people, from warehouse workers to C-suite executives, advance their careers through improved communication skills and greater self-confidence. With degrees in international communication and languages, as well as advanced studies in training and development, she has been providing communication training in Singapore since 2006. She is a recognised authority on proper pronunciation, English language use, public speaking and interpersonal skills.

This is Heather's first book. It presents her winning approach to interpersonal communication, which is deeply rooted in a firm belief in lifelong learning, a conviction that 'being yourself' is the best place to start building people skills, and a commitment to bringing out the very best in every individual.

Heather believes that all learning should be fun, personalised and practical. Her clear, no-nonsense writing style captures much of the energy that has made her so sought after as a speaker and trainer.

Although originally from the United States, Heather has spent most of her adult life abroad, living and working in several countries in Europe and Asia. She currently lives with her husband and daughter in Singapore, where she runs her own successful company, Hansen Speech & Language Training.

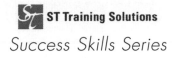 **ST Training Solutions**

Success Skills Series

ST Training Solutions, based in Singapore, offers a wide range of popular, practical training programmes conducted by experienced, professional trainers. As CEO, Shirley Taylor takes a personal interest in working closely with trainers to ensure that each workshop is full of valuable tools, helpful guidelines and powerful action steps that will ensure a true learning experience for all participants. Some of the workshops offered are:

Power up your Business Writing Skills
Energise your E-mail Writing Skills
Success Skills for Secretaries and Support Staff
Successful Business Communication Skills
Creativity at Work
Present for Success
Speak up Successfully
Powerful People Skills
Get to Grips with Grammar
Activate your Listening Skills
Emotional Intelligence at Work
Business Etiquette and Professional Poise
Dealing with Difficult People and Situations
Achieving Peak Performance by Improving your Memory
Embrace your Productivity with Speed-reading
Personal Effectiveness and You
Projecting a Professional Image

Shirley Taylor is also host of a very popular annual conference called ASSAP — the Asian Summit for Secretaries and Admin Professionals — organised in April each year by ST Training Solutions.

Find out more about ST Training Solutions at www.shirleytaylortraining.com. Visit www.STSuccessSkills.com for additional resources.